MEDIA, FEMINISM, CULTURAL STUDIES

Stepping Forward: Essays, Lectures and Interviews
by Wolfgang Iser

Wild Zones: Pornography, Art and Feminism
by Kelly Ives

Global Media Warning: Explorations of Radio, Television and the Press
by Oliver Whitehorne

'Cosmo Woman': The World of Women's Magazines
by Oliver Whitehorne

Andrea Dworkin
by Jeremy Mark Robinson

Cixous, Irigaray, Kristeva: The Jouissance of French Feminism
by Kelly Ives

Sex in Art: Pornography and Pleasure in Painting and Sculpture
by Cassidy Hughes

The Erotic Object: Sexuality in Sculpture
From Prehistory to the Present Day
by Susan Quinnell

Women in Pop Music
by Helen Challis

Detonation Britain: Nuclear War in the UK
by Jeremy Mark Robinson

Julia Kristeva: Art, Love, Melancholy, Philosophy, Semiotics
by Kelly Ives

Luce Irigaray: Lips, Kissing, and the Politics of Sexual Difference
by Kelly Ives

Helene Cixous I Love You: The Jouissance of Writing
by Kelly Ives

The Poetry of Cinema
by John Madden

The Sacred Cinema of Andrei Tarkovsky
by Jeremy Mark Robinson

Disney Business, Disney Films, Disney Lands
Daniel Cerruti

Feminism and Shakespeare
by B.D. Barnacle

Thomas Hardy's *Jude the Obscure*

A Critical Study

Thomas Hardy's *Jude the Obscure*
A Critical Study

Margaret Elvy

CRESCENT MOON

CRESCENT MOON PUBLISHING
P.O. Box 393
Maidstone
Kent, ME14 5XU
United Kingdom

First published 2000. Second edition 2008.
© Margaret Elvy 2000, 2008.

Printed and bound in Great Britain.
Set in Book Antiqua 9 on 14pt and Gill Sans display.
Designed by Radiance Graphics.

The right of Margaret Elvy to be identified as the author of *Thomas Hardy's Jude the Obscure* has been asserted generally in accordance with sections 77 and 78 of the Copyright, Designs and Patents Act 1988.

British Library Cataloguing in Publication data

Elvy, Margaret
Thomas Hardy's Jude the Obscure: A Critical Study. –
(Thomas Hardy Studies Series; v. 6)
1. Hardy, Thomas, 1840-1928. Jude the Obscure
I. Title
823.8

ISBN 1-86171-121-2
ISBN-13 978-1-86171-121-2

CONTENTS

ABBREVIATIONS

J	*Jude the Obscure*
T	*Tess of the D'Urbervilles*
R	*The Return of the Native*
W	*The Woodlanders*
M	*The Mayor of Casterbridge*
F	*Far From the Madding Crowd*
U	*Under the Greenwood Tree*
PBE	*A Pair of Blue Eyes*
WB	*The Well-Beloved*
TT	*Two on a Tower*
Lao	*A Laocidean*
DR	*Desperate Remedies*
HE	*The Hand of Ethelberta*
TM	*The Trumpet-Major*
D	*The Dynasts*
CP	*Complete Poems*
Love	*Hardy's Love Poems*
SS	*The Short Stories of Thomas Hardy*
Lit	*The Literary Notebooks of Thomas Hardy*
Let	*The Collected Letters of Thomas Hardy*
Per	*The Personal Notebooks of Thomas Hardy*
L	*The Life and Work of Thomas Hardy*
PW	*Personal Writings*
H	*The Sense of Sex*, ed. Margaret Higonnet

Thomas Hardy's *Jude the Obscure*

A Critical Study

Thomas Hardy's birthplace in Dorset
(Photo: Jeremy Robinson, 1997)

Jude's beloved Oxford, in a J.M.W. Turner watercolour from 1793, *Oxford: St Mary's From Oriel Lane* (Clore Gallery, London)

I

Introductory:
The Thomas Hardy Myth

A mass of critical data has grown up around Thomas Hardy. He is one of the most discussed authors in the language. This sample from John Peck is typical of the kind of Hardy criticism which sees in his work a marvellous evocation of hidden emotions, often vaguely called the unconscious:

> *Hardy offers us something more exciting than a mirror image of life… he always writes with a sense of a force which is elusive and cannot be explained… his most extraordinary ability is to create and convey a sense of a natural energy at work in life.* (J. Peck, 59)

One could also cite Thomas Hardy critics such as Gregor, Bayley, Millgate, Howe, Cecil, Larkin, Auden and a host of others as producing similar criticism. Hardy has had it easy, as far as most criticism is concerned. The collections of essays and criticism (such as those edited by Guerard, Smith, Butler, Kramer, Draper and Mallett, the stalwarts of any public or college library) were sincere efforts, but hardly ever offered something other than humanist, formal, and often vague criticism. Even in the 1980s and 1990s books on Thomas Hardy kept coming out which preferred not to acknowledge writers such as Jacques Derrida, Gilles Deleuze, Felix Guattari, Paul de Man, Jean Baudrillard, Mikhail Bakhtin, Jacques Lacan, Annette Kuhn, Laura Mulvey or feminist thinkers such as Julia Kristeva, Luce Irigaray, Gayatri Chakravorty Spivak, Linda Williams, Monique Wittig, Adrienne Rich, Alice Jardine, bell hooks, Judith Butler, Teresa de Lauretis and Elizabeth Grosz.

The two most perceptive collections of essays on Thomas Hardy up to the mid-1990s were edited by L. Butler (1989) and M. Higonnet (1993). After Derrida and deconstruction, to take one kind of post-1960s criticism, texts were no longer 'whole', but were, in the words of an important Hardy critic (J. Hillis Miller), 'undecidable'. Texts were 'self-subverting', in the process of dismantling themselves, leading to a multiplicity of sometimes conflicting readings.[1] As a mid-1990s book of feminist criticism said, a heterogeneity of theoretical positions seems to be inevitable (S. Mills, 1994, 283).

Where critics have a field day demolishing Thomas Hardy's art is in his literary style in his fiction. Hardy's style at its worst is marked by 'verbosity and redundance, with ponderous words, clumsily poly-syllabic, and unhappy phrases' (I. Baker, 95). Hardy's deliberate complexity or learned allusions do sometimes make his fiction very creaky and ugly. Occasionally, he *is* really bad, so the reader cringes. Often the failures in style occur in lulls between events, for when some dramatic event is taking place, such as the storm over the ricks in *Far From the Madding Crowd*, Hardy's narration is tremendous (but then, only a terrible writer couldn't make a storm work in writing).

Many of the books on Hardy's fiction stay safe and discuss his Wessex, or his nature poetry, the 'Thomas Hardy' of a rural, nostalgic and now lost world (Kay-Robinson, Lea, Williams, Sherren, Windle). In this view, 'Hardy' is the 'tragic novelist of character struggling heroically with nature, Fate, or other, pre-eminently non-social forces' (P. Widdowson, 1983, 13). This is the 'Thomas Hardy' the tourist and TV industries promulgate, the 'Thomas Hardy' of expensive television adaptions and tourist board brochures. Hélène Cixous writes that 'the mystery is that we confuse invent and believe.'[2] This is worth keeping in mind, especially with regard to Hardy's characters, who seem so 'real', so that Hardy fans, visiting modern day Marnhull in North Dorset, think they are beholding Tess's 'real' cottage.

Julia Kristeva's description of the 'writer' is quite different from that imagined by newspaper columnists working for the middlebrow Sunday supplements, or visitors to the local public library, or most Hardy critics:

> I shall term "writer" that ability to rebound whereby the violence of rejection, in extravagant rhythm, finds its way into a multiplied signifier. It is not the reconstruction of a unwary subject, reminiscing, in hysterical fashion, about his lacks in meaning, his plunges into an underwater body. It is rather the return of the limit-as-break, castration, and the bar separating signifier from signified, which found naming, codification, and language; they do this not in order to vanish at that point (as communal meaning would have it), but in order, lucidly and consciously, to reject and multiply them, to dissolve even their boundaries, and to use them again. (Desire in Language, 187)

Much of Thomas Hardy criticism is of the humanist, formal, New Criticism ilk, taking Hardy's texts as the products of one person (Howe, Stewart, Cecil, Bayley, Abercrombie, Woolf, Kay-Robinson, Brooks, Millgate, Pinion, Alvarez, Gatrell, Draper, Beach, Blunden, Davie, Williams, Gregor, Guerard). These were the critics that helped put Hardy into the centre of English literature. Few critics had anything new to say about Hardy's fiction that had not already been said by the 1950s.

Thomas Hardy has had one or two critics that have produced startling work, the most obvious is perhaps D.H. Lawrence, whose *A Study of Thomas Hardy* has provoked much critical debate. Indeed, there is a section of Hardy (meta)criticism devoted to Lawrence on Hardy.

It was surprising, perhaps, that F.R. Leavis left Thomas Hardy out of his Great Tradition. It is odd that Leavis exalted George Eliot and D.H. Lawrence, but not Thomas Hardy. Leavis grudgingly acknowledged the greatness of a dozen of Hardy's poems, but his novels were vastly overrated, Leavis reckoned.[3] Hardy's work, though, had far too many other critics championing it to be much affected by Leavis's omission.

Another 'Thomas Hardy's beloved of critics is the philosopher, pessimist and sometime Buddhist (authors such as Garwood, Grimditch,

Butler, Braybrooke, Elliott, Southerington, Brennecke, Sherman and Chandra Dave have written of Hardy's 'philosophy'). This is the 'Thomas Hardy' that became an Existentialist in the 1950s, an inheritor of the German philosophy of Arthur Schopenhauer and Friedrich Nietzsche, a dramatist in the Theatre of the Absurd of Eugene Ionesco, Antonin Artaud and Samuel Beckett.

Thomas Hardy's biographers have not greatly altered his critical status, whether the biographies have been 'sympathetic' (M. Millgate, R. Purdy, F. Pinion, F. Halliday), or seen as potentially damaging (M. Seymour-Smith, Gittings). There have been too few critical views of Hardy's works that use materialism, Marxism, deconstructionism, psychoanalysis, feminism or postmodernism. Critics who have employed some of the more recent critical approaches, loosely termed 'cultural theory', include Hillis Miller, Butler, Goode, Ebbatson, Lecercle, R. Saldivar, Eagleton, Widdowson, Janie Sénéchal-Teissedou, Lock, Tanner and Wootton. Critics I would cite as particularly enriching, not including the feminist critics (see below), include Widdowson, Lecercle, Lawrence and Goode, and to a lesser extent, Ebbatson, Tanner and Eagleton.

One might suppose that Tom Hardy's work has been particularly well-served by feminist criticism – there seems to have been a lot of it (Boumelha, Woolf, Stubbs, Rogers, Showalter, Miles, Morgan, Sumner, Ingham, Wright, Jacobus, Millett, Williams and Garson). 'Probably no male author in English literature has been the subject of so much feminist appraisal' wrote Charles Lock (1992, 126). I would disagree: D.H. Lawrence has had just as much attention from feminists, and Lawrence feminist criticism has generally been of a higher quality. And so had Shakespeare

Feminist critics have been interested by the feminism-in-the-making in Hardy's fiction, and by his female characters.[4] Hardy says a lot about the human, and feminine predicament. His texts manage, through an impressionist approach, to make people 'enlarged and dignified', as Virginia Woolf put it. Hardy's ability to dignify and elevate people is partly what makes him 'the greatest tragic writer among English novelists' (1932, 253f). Much of Hardy criticism is masculinist and sexist, like most literary criticism from the ancient Greeks onwards. However, except in a few cases (Mary Jacobus, Linda Williams and Rosemarie Morgan), most feminist Hardy criticism is usually of the well-trodden second wave feminist type, as epitomized by Kate Millet's *Sexual Politics*. Laudable as the attempts of most feminist critics are, their insights into Hardy's work remain limited and disappointing (Rosemary Sumner, Rosalind Miles, Elaine Showalter, Penny Boumelha, Patricia Stubbs, Katherine Rogers and Patricia Ingham). Far and away the best collection of feminist approaches to Hardy's work, and one of the very best books on Hardy, is *The Sense of Sex*, (ed. Margaret Higonnet, 1993).

Thomas Hardy divided up his novels into three groups, and Hardy critics have kept, by and large, to the divisions ever since. The six 'great'/ 'tragic' Hardy novels are *Tess of the d'Urbervilles, Jude the Obscure, The Return of the Native, The Mayor of Casterbridge, Far From the Madding Crowd* and *The Woodlanders*. This is the central group of novels that is discussed in nearly every book on Hardy. It corresponds to Hardy's 'Novels of Character and Environment'. Hardy criticism next groups together the 'minor' or 'secondary' novels, which come from the category 'Romances and Fantasies': *Two On a Tower, A Pair of Blue Eyes, The Trumpet-Major, The Well-Beloved* and *Under the Greenwood Tree* (this latter is in Hardy's first group, though hardly any Hardy critic puts it beside *Tess* or *Jude*). This middle group of 'lesser' novels is usually discussed in Hardy criticism, often dealt with in one chapter, with the major novels having a chapter each. The short stories are usually analyzed in the 'minor works' chapter: *Life's Little Ironies, Wessex Tales* and *A Group of Noble Dames*. Then come the novels which are rarely discussed anywhere: *The Hand of Ethelberta, Desperate Remedies* and *A Laodicean*. It is assumed (wrongly, perhaps) that the 'lesser' novels, such as *A Laodicean* and *Desperate Remedies*, have too many faults to make them 'great' or worthy of discussion.

2

Thomas Hardy and Feminism

What are my books but one long plea against 'man's inhumanity to man' – to woman – and to the lower animals? Whatever may be the inherent good or evil of life, it is certain that men make it much worse than it need be.

Thomas Hardy, 1904 (in F. Pinion, 1968, 178)

Is Thomas Hardy a feminist? Are Thomas Hardy's works feminist? How much do his works reflect and bolster the patriarchal attitudes and values of his era, and how much do they question them? What is the relation between Hardy and the feminists of his time? And what is the relation between Hardy's works and the feminism of the early 21st century? These are interrelated questions. We are concerned here with Thomas Hardy's novels, not the man or author himself, and the fictions' relations with contemporary feminism. When we write Hardy we mean the 'Hardy' that is written into the novels, the 'Hardy' who is and is not the narrator of the novels.[1] We mean the 'Hardy' created by the texts, not the biographical, 'real' 'Hardy' who lived at Max Gate in Dorchester, who had certain literary and wealthy friends, who went up to London for 'the season', who bicycled around Dorset, who was fond of pet dogs.[2] Instead of there being a direct connection between author and reader, which humanist criticism assumes, there can be seen as at least six levels of mediation: real author > implied author > narrator > narratee > implied reader > real reader.[2] The 'real reader' is thus at a critical distance from the 'real author', 'Thomas Hardy'.

Thomas Hardy's theme is 'Wessexuality', 'Wes-sex-mania', Wessexual politics. Thomas Hardy's works are sexist, patriarchal and masculinist, and yet they question notions of sexism, gender, identity, subjectivity, patriarchy and masculinism.[3] A text such as *Tess of the d'Urbervilles* is 'traditional', and follows patriarchal codes and morals. Yet it also questions them, and offers a number of feminist critiques of late 19th century society. In his letters Hardy proposed feminist views; he wrote to feminists such as the suffragette leader Millicent Fawcett that a child was the mother's own business, not the father's (*Collected Letters*, 3, 238). One can see these feminist sentiments in, for example, Hardy's treatment of Tess Durbeyfield in her motherhood: she works in the fields just a few weeks after the birth, even though she is melancholy (she seems to be suffering a mild form of post-natal depression). Tess further subverts patriarchy by taking her child's baptism into her own hands. She goes against her father, the vicar, and the whole church with her self-made baptism.

Donald Hall offers a typical (male) critical response to *Tess of the d'Urbervilles*: 'Hardy was clearly in love with Tess, and he leaves his male readers in the same condition.'[4] Rosalind Miles' view of Hardy and women is typical of the second wave feminist criticism ('womanist' is a better term) which was pro-Hardy. For Miles, Hardy had an intuitive and exalted view of women:

> He had, surely, a deeply intuitive under-standing of female nature... Hardy's guileless and ecstatic response to women in life irradiated his writing at every possible level... For Hardy really is a lover of women in the fullest physical sense. (1979, 25-26).

For some feminists, Hardy did not necessarily 'like' women, as (male) critics such as Irving Howe claimed (M. Childers, 1981).

A typical 'feminist' analysis of Thomas Hardy's work comes from Elaine Showalter. In "Towards a Feminist Poetics" (1979), Showalter offers a rather simplistic analysis of the wife-selling scene in *The Mayor of Casterbridge*. She takes as her departure point one of the archetypal humanist studies of Hardy, Irving Howe's *Thomas Hardy* (1968).

> *What Howe, like other male critics of Hardy, conveniently overlooks about the novel is that Henchard sells not only his wife but his child, a child who can only be female. Patriarchal societies do not readily sell their sons, but their daughters are all for sale sooner or later.* (in M. Jacobus, 26f)

Showalter's analysis is in the same sort of vein as the feminism in Kate Millett's *Sexual Politics*. Millett's book deconstructed writers such as Henry Miller, Norman Mailer and D.H. Lawrence, exposing the sexist assumptions in their books. Millett's analysis, though, like much of Anglo-American feminism, is distinctly humanist, and modernist, assuming that whatever is in the text relates directly to the author, that whatever is in the text is there deliberately and consciously. This kind of Anglo-American feminism assumes that the text is transparent, so that if a text appears misogynist, then that writer is misogynist.

French feminism, cultural studies and postmodern feminism, however, does not regard the text as transparent, and departs dramatically from humanist criticism at many key points. Humanist feminism talks of Thomas Hardy, but postmodern or cultural theory feminism talks of 'Thomas Hardy', that is, a writer who is 'written' by the social, ideological, cultural, materialist and economic forces around 'him'. Feminism of the type of Millett, Showalter, Miles *et al* essentializes Hardy's female characters: this view of Rosalind Miles' is typical: '[f]or Hardy, femininity was a value, an essence, an eternal and inescapable fact' (1979, 43), which's patently untrue. Showalter's Anglo-American feminist analysis, then, is strong on simple assertions, but short on subtle, ironic, thoughtful insights. Showalter, for example, asserts:

> *Hardy's female characters in* **The Mayor of Casterbridge,** *as in his other novels, are somewhat idealised and melancholy projections of a repressed male self.* (ib., 26f)

Showalter assumes a direct line back from the character to the author. Roland Barthes has called for the 'death of the author', where the idea of the author who suffers for the book, who 'nourishes' the book, is discarded in favour of a notion of writing as a 'multi-dimensional space in which a variety of writings, none of them original, blend and clash' (R. Barthes, 1984, 144f). In cultural theory, 'writing' or 'literature' is multi-dimensional, with an infinity of possible readings. Linearity is discarded, and texts continually change. Nothing is fixed anymore, and meanings fluctuate.

Thomas Hardy's women are known and yet not known – by the reader (and, one suspects, by the narrator). Rather than getting to know the women in Hardy's novels, the reader gets to know Hardy's narrator (and perhaps Hardy himself).[5] Female characters such as Tess, Eustacia, Sue and Bathsheba, seem to have a substantial and subtle subjectivity, but, as Judith Mitchel argues, their subjecthood is 'largely illusory' (ib., 179). Hardy's narrators offer detailed physical descriptions of the female characters, but leaves out much of their thoughts. This is part of Hardy's narrational project, but it can also be seen as 'a glaring omission of female consciousness' (ib., 183). Hardy, via his narrators, gets up close and lovingly describes his heroines' physical features (most famously Tess's mouth), but his narrator are also oddly distanced from his characters. Consequently, Hardy's heroines remain mysterious, always partially unknowable by the reader.

There are moments, for example, when the reader would expect to find out what a female character is thinking: when Eustacia Vye is wandering the Heath just before her death, or Tess's feelings after she has killed Alec. Even in more mundane, less dramatic moments, such as when Marty puts down her billhook at the beginning of *The Woodlanders* and looks at her blistered hand, when the reader might expect to find out what she is thinking, the narrative moves into a more general voice.[6]

Patricia Stubbs pointed out that Thomas Hardy was ambivalent about his female characters, not always condemning the social pressures and psychological characteristics that contributed towards women's suffering (1979, 81f). Penny Boumelha reckoned that the radicalism of Hardy's depictions of women did not reside in their 'complexity' or 'realism' but 'in their resistance to a single and uniform ideological position' (1982, 7).

Hardy's novels were not always received favourably by women critics and readers. Hardy's own views, expressed outside of the novels, did not always square with those of feminists of the 1880s and 1890s. The ideological gap between Hardy and the women critics and feminists of the late 19th century is illustrated by Hardy's remark to Edmund Yates (in 1891): 'many of my novels have suffered so much from misrepresentation as being attacks on womankind.' (*Collected Letters*, I, 250) Hardy hoped that works such as *Tess of the d'Urbervilles* would redress the balance.

In Tom Hardy's fiction, as in so much of literature (certainly in the works of James Joyce, Norman Mailer, Henry Miller, D.H. Lawrence, Virginia Woolf, Gertrude Stein, Philip Roth, J.P. Donleavy) women and men are at odds with each other. The connection between men and women in fiction is always fraught with conflict. Luce Irigaray suggests a fundamental *difference* between the sexes: '[m]an and woman, woman and man are therefore always meeting as though for the first time since they cannot stand in for one another. I shall never take the place of a man, never will a man take mine.'[7] A politics of sexual union between men and women has still not been created, Irigaray suggests, because there is no continuity between the spiritual and material, the sacred and the sexual aspects of life.

Irigaray writes:

> A sexual or carnal ethics would demand that both angel and body be found together. This is a world that must be constructed or reconstructed. A genesis of love between the sexes has yet to come about, in either the smallest or largest sense, or in the most intimate or political guise. (in ib., 127)

For Irigaray, as for Rainer Maria Rilke, the angel is the emblem or manifestation of a fluid openness, the angel is the one who opens up life, who circulates between God and humanity. One sees the 'angel' beginning to appear in *anima* or Sophia characters such as Sue Bridehead.

You have to consider exactly what character is – a function of the text?

What is the relation between character and text? A character is interpreted differently by everyone: how is a character constructed in the minds of different readers? What are the factors, 'inside' and 'outside' the text, that govern character?

THOMAS HARDY AND SEXUAL DIFFERENCE

Lesbian, gay and queer cultural theory has continually addressed the problem of identity and gender. There are certain sexual and social 'positions' or 'categories' which are seen as 'outside' the (patriarchal) norms, which may have affinities with the female 'outsider' figures of Julia Kristeva and Luce Irigaray. The lesbian, for instance, is sometimes seen as an 'outsider', like the black woman, or the feminist. Gender and sexual identity categories are becoming increasingly blurred. For example, there are 'physical' lesbians, 'natural' lesbians, 'cultural' or 'social' lesbians, and 'male' lesbians (men who culturally position themselves as lesbians). There are men with vaginas and women with penises; there are queer butches and aggressive femmes, there are F2Ms and lesbians who love men, queer queens and drag kings, daddy boys and dyke mummies, transsexual Asians, butch bottoms, femme tops, women and lesbians who fuck men, women and lesbians who fuck *like* men, bull daggers, porno afro homos, lesbians who dress up as men impersonating women, lesbians who dress up as straight men in order to pick up gay men, butches who dress in fem clothing to feel like a gay man dressing as a woman, femmes butched-out in male drag and butches femmed-out in drag. Sexual/ social identities are continually being performed, blurred, re-defined, questioned. Terms such as 'straight' and 'gay', hetero and homo/ hommo, are no longer adequate for these multi-layered, postmodern sexual identities. As Judith Halberstamp puts it '[w]e are all transsexuals'.[8]

Some feminists regard sexuality as expressed through performances and gestures, rather than being some essence. Thus heterosexuality itself is not an unchanging 'institution', but may already be a 'constant parody of itself', as Judith Butler suggests (1990, 122). Heterosexuality, Butler reckons, is continually imitating itself, always miming its own performances in order to appear 'natural'. Further, if gender, sexuality and forms of sexuality such as heterosexuality are simulations and performances, the notion of a fixed, essentialist 'man' or 'woman' is no longer possible.9 Catherine MacKinnon wrote: '[s]exuality is that social process which creates, organizes, expresses, and directs desire, creating the social beings we know as women and men, as their relations create society.'10 Adrienne Rich, in her influential essay "Compulsory heterosexuality and lesbian existence", says that heterosexuality is not 'preferred' or chosen, but has to be 'imposed, managed, organized, propagandized, and maintained by force'; for Rich, 'violent structures' are required by patriarchal society in order to 'enforce women's total emotional, erotic loyalty and subservience to men' (1980).

Thomas Hardy's female protagonists can be seen as characters struggling to attain coherent social and sexual identity, to become an independent body and soul, someone who can exist independently of a patriarchal culture. Critics have noted that figures such as Sue Bridehead are versions of the late Victorian 'New Woman'. Indeed, Sue proposes a number of feminist views, and *Jude the Obscure* is an early feminist work, in which relationships between the sexes and notions of gender are examined in the light of what Hardy might call 'progressive' philosophy. In *Jude the Obscure*, more than in any of his other works, Hardy grapples with the notion of an emergent 'New Woman', and a heartfelt proto-feminism.11 At the same time, so-called 'New Woman' fiction was already going out of fashion when *Jude the Obscure* was published (1895); also, the 'New Woman' was not wholly feminist (P. Boumelha, 1982, 136-7).

One can see some of Hardy's other female protagonists as would-be feminists, as women struggling against patriarchy.12 Each, in their own way, is trying to affirm her identity in the face of patriarchy. Tess, Marty, Eustacia, Elizabeth-Jane and Sue question, not always in obvious or outspoken ways, the rigours of patriarchy. Characters such as Tess,

Eustacia, Sue and Elizabeth-Jane, in particular, are forms of 'woman' as 'outsider' figures who inhabit what feminists term 'the wild zone'. It's not perhaps surprising that Thomas Hardy should be so close to some aspects of contemporary feminism, in particular the notion of 'woman' as one of the marginalized, dispossessed people.

Feminists such as Elaine Showalter and Jeanne Roberts, taking their cue from Edwin Ardener,[13] propose that there is a female 'wild zone', as there is a male 'wild zone'. We know about men's version of wild zone eroticism, it's the place of 'glorious phallic monosexuality', in Hélène Cixous' words.[14] The female 'wild zone' is beyond patriarchal space, beyond patriarchal representations.[15] Julia Kristeva and Luce Irigaray, among other French feminists, have spoken of something in 'women' or the 'feminine' that is 'unrepresentable', beyond art, beyond male culture. In *About Chinese Women*, Kristeva writes of the woman as a witch, someone outside of patriarchal discourse, or at least, thrown to the edge, the border between the known zone and the wild zone:

> *…woman is a specialist in the unconscious, a witch, a bacchanalian, taking her* jouissance *in an anti-Apollonian, Dionysian orgy. A* jouissance *which breaks the symbolic chain, the taboo, the mastery. A* marginal discourse, *with regard to the science, religion and philosophy of the* polis *(witch, child, underdeveloped, not even a poet, at best his accomplice). (The Kristeva Reader,* **154**)

Tess Durbeyfield is called a 'witch' by Alec, but the meaning here is witch = whore (the 'Witch of Babylon'). Eustacia Vye is not only likened to a witch, she is physically attacked by Susan Nonsuch, who pierces her in church with a needle, echoing the 'pricking' of witches in mediæval times. Sherry Ortner writes that 'woman is being identified with – or, if you will, seems to be a symbol of – something that every culture devalues'.[16] Ann Rosalind Jones describes Julia Kristeva's notion of the 'outsider' culture of women, of women as 'witches':

> *Women, for Kristev.… speak and write as "hysterics," as outsiders to male-dominated discourse, for two reasons: the predominance in them of drives related to anality and childbirth, and their marginal position vis-à-vis masculine culture. Their semiotic style is likely to involve repetitive,*

spasmodic separations from the dominating discourse, which, more often, they are forced to imitate.[17]

Julia Kristeva's writings may be the most coherent and incisive account of the psycho-cultural 'wild zone'. Victor Burgin, describing Kristeva's philosophy, says that she positions

the woman in society… in the patriarchal, as perpetually at the boundary, the borderline, the edge, the 'outer limit' – the place where order shades into chaos, light into darkness. The peripheral and ambivalent position allocated to woman, says Kristeva, had led to that familiar division of the field of representation in which women are viewed as either saintly or demonic – according to whether they are seen as bringing the darkness in, or as keeping it out.[18]

Saintly woman (the Virgin Mary is a typical example) keeps the amazing energy of the female wild zone out of men's lives; the demonic woman (Mary Magdalene, the *femme fatale*, vampire, 'devil woman') is the one who brings the wildness with her. Patriarchy of course prefers bland, mute, passive door-stops in women, people who will stop the darkness from coming in, who will sit there and say nothing and get on with society's housework. For Julia Kristeva, Christianity offers a limited number of ways in which women can participate in the 'symbolic Christian order': for the woman who is not a virgin or a nun (like Hardy's heroines), who is sexual, has orgasms and gives birth

her only means of gaining access to the symbolic paternal order is by engaging in an endless struggle between the orgasmic maternal body and the symbolic prohibition – a struggle that will take the form of guilt and mortification, and culminates in masochistic jouissance. *For a woman who has not easily repressed her relationship with her mother, participation in the symbolic paternal order as Christianity defines it can only be masochistic.* (1986, 147)

This applies to Thomas Hardy's characters such as Sue Bridehead and Tess. Two of the classic ways in which women have been allowed to participate in Christianity is the '*ecstatic* and the *melancholy*' (ib.).

André Breton said that 'existence is elsewhere'. French feminists say that 'woman' is elsewhere. 'She is indefinitely other in herself,' writes Luce Irigaray, maintaining that women

> *are already elsewhere than in the discursive machinery where you claim to take them by surprise. They have turned back within themselves, which does not mean the same thing as 'within yourself'. They do not experience the same interiority that you do and which perhaps you mistakenly presume they share.'*[19]

Here, perhaps, in the female 'wild zone', some of the wildness and strangeness and ecstasy of 'female' eroticism may be experienced and depicted. Luce Irigaray also spoke in spatial terms of idealist feminism (it's all about labia for Irigaray):

> *We need both space and time. And perhaps we are living in an age when time must re-deploy space. Could this be the dawning of a new world? Immanence and transcendence are being recast, notably by that threshold which has never been examined in itself: the female sex. It is a threshold unto mucosity. Beyond the classic opposites of love and hate, liquid and ice lies this perpetually half-open threshold, consisting of lips that are strangers to dichotomy. Pressed against one another, but without any possibility of suture, at least of a real kind, they do not absorb the world either into themselves or through themselves, provided they are not abused or reduced to a mere consummating or consuming structure. Instead their shape welcomes without assimilating or reducing or devouring. A sort of door unto voluptuousness, then? Not that, either: their useful function is to designate a place: the very place of uses, at least on a habitual plane. Strictly speaking, they serve neither conception nor jouissance. Is this, then, the mystery of female identity, of its self-contemplation, of that strange word of silence; both the threshold and reception of exchange, the sealed-up secret of wisdom, belief and faith in every truth?*[20]

For some feminists, Luce Irigaray's morphology of female creativity is empowering, 'a challenge to the traditional construction of feminine morphology where the bodies of women are seen as receptacles for masculine completeness.'[21] Other feminists see the emphasis on just one form of female sexuality as a distinctly reductive and inauthentic kind of feminism:

> *If we define female subjectivity through universal biological/ libidinal*

givens [writes Ann Rosalind Jones], what happens to the project of changing the world in feminist directions? Further, is women's sexuality so monolithic that shared, typical femininity does justice to it? What about variations in class, in race, and in culture among women? about changes over time in one woman's sexuality? (with men, with women, by herself?) How can one libidinal voice – or the two vulval lips so startlingly presented by Irigaray – speak for all women? (1986, 369)

Many feminists suggest that women's eroticism cannot be represented, much as women themselves cannot be represented. Julia Kristeva writes: '[i]n "woman" I see something that cannot be represented, something that is not said, something above and beyond nomenclatures and ideologies.'[22] Other feminists echo this idea, that women cannot be fully represented in the traditional media of patriarchy. As Hélène Cixous writes:

It is at the level of sexual pleasure in my opinion that the difference makes itself most clearly apparent in as far as woman's libidinal economy is neither identifiable by a man nor referable to the masculine economy.[23]

The unrepresentable in art and pornography, according to some feminists, is women's eroticism, their *jouissance*, that 'explosive, blossoming, sane and inexhaustible *jouissance* of the woman', as Julia Kristeva describes it.[24]

What we get in most Western art, from Greek and Roman sculpture through the glories of the Renaissance to the latest pornography are male representations of female eroticism. Feminists say that there are no real depictions of female *jouissance* in art or literature. 'In my opinion,' writes Marguerite Duras, 'women have never expressed themselves.'[25] What she means, perhaps, is that women have expressed themselves thus far in terms and means defined by men. There is no 'feminine' or 'women's' writing, according to some feminists. Hélène Cixous reckons she's found only three 'inscriptions of femininity' this century: Sidonie-Gabrielle Colette, Marguerite Duras and Jean Genet.[26]

The point is *not* to consider bodies as essential or absolute, for 'no "body" is unmediated'.[27] In *écriture féminine* the body is a major source of creative energy, so that 'to write from the body is to re-create the world' (A. Jones, 1986, 366). Real sex, the French feminists argue, has not yet been represented. Women haven't done it because they work within the same patriarchal structures, codes and constraints as men. Men, generally, haven't got a hope of depicting authentic 'female' eroticism, although the authors of millions of pornographic products would claim they know everything about 'female' eroticism. On the other hand, in the mechanisms of cultural/ postmodern theory, anyone, male or female, should be able to create a truly 'feminine' text. It shouldn't matter who the author is. If the French feminists are right, then nearly all of the art produced anywhere is orientated to the male and the masculine, even when it is created by women. Many women artists would dispute this. The notion of an 'authentic' 'women's'/ 'feminine' art continues to be hotly debated.

According to the French feminists, 'women's' or 'feminine' or 'female' art is created in the gaps and silences of a text, but not in the intentional space of the artwork. Mary Jacobus explains:

> The French insistence on écriture féminine – on woman as a writing-effect instead of an origin – asserts not the sexuality of the text but the textuality of sex. Gender difference, produced, not innate, becomes a matter of the structuring of a genderless libido in and through patriarchal discourse. Language itself would at once repress multiplicity and heterogeneity – true difference – by the tyranny of hierarchical oppositions (man/woman) and simultaneously work to overthrow that tyranny by interrogating the limits of meaning. The 'feminine', in this scheme, is to be located in the gaps, the absences, the unsayable or unrepresentable of discourse and repre-sentation.[28]

Some feminist critics, such as Gayatri Chakravorty Spivak and Emma Pérez, believe that 'representation cannot take place without essential-ism'.[29] For some feminists, philosophies based on the body are problematic, because to look for some essential nature of 'woman', some essence based in biology is dubious.[30] Indeed, Toril Moi writes that 'to define 'woman' is necessarily to essentialize her.'[31] What is 'woman', anyway? A 'writing-effect', for the feminist Alice Jardine, an element in culture or a text. It's important, as Monique Wittig notes, to make a distinction between the various interpretations 'woman' and 'women':

> Our first task… is thoroughly to dissociate "woman" (the class within which we fight) and "woman," the myth. For "woman" does not exist for

us; it is only an imaginary formation, while "women" is the duct of a social relationship.[32]

Sue and Jude's non-marital state disrupts the conventional notions of sexual relationships in late 19th century society. There are even more disruptive erotic relationships possible, though, such as homosexuality and lesbiansim. Even more potentially 'subversive', as far as hetero-patriarchy is concerned, are lesbian motherhood, or sexual represent-ations between crossdressing, transvestite or transsexual partners.

There is no erotic relationship in Hardy's fiction that approaches such unorthodoxy or fucking with gender, and there's only one representation that's seen as 'lesbian' by Hardy critics (Miss Aldclyffe and Cytherea Graye in *Desperate Remedies*). Describing Miss Aldclyffe's reaction to Cytherea helping her undress, a (male) Hardy critic says that Miss Aldclyffe's rigid body and firmly closed mouth 'is how a forty-six-year-old sexually excited woman in such a situation would behave' (M. Seymour-Smith, 1995, 129). What a ridiculous pronouncement.

There are other relationships between women which Thomas Hardy critics, if coaxed, might admit have some lesbian elements: Grace and Felice lost in the woods and clinging to each other, their dialogue becoming more and more intimate; and Tess and the 'sisterhood' at Talbothays and Marlott. 'When women use *je* as the subject of a sentence, this woman *je* most often addresses a man and not another woman or women. It does not relate to itself either' writes Luce Irigaray (1994, 46). Gay male eroticism can be discerned in many of the friendships in Hardy's fiction. This often occurs when lovers of the same woman meet and commune in the 'trade' of women between men that Luce Irigaray identified (Wildeve and Venn; Oak and Boldwood). In Hardy's fiction, only mild forms of 'gender-play', 'gender bending', 'gender-fucking' or 'fucking with gender' occur.[33]

The sexual relations in Thomas Hardy's fiction overwhelmingly conform to the heteropatriarchal model. Anything non-monogamous or adulterous is viewed with horror by some parts of the Wessex community. What is surprising, perhaps, is the number of feminists in the early 21st century who also believed in (heterosexual) monogamy as the goal. Even for some radical feminists, lovers still have to be wholly committed to monogamy.[34] Men must not be interested in other women. They are not even allowed to look at pictures of naked women – this is seen as tantamount to adultery. 'I should be everything for him', the devoted wife complains when she finds pornography in her husband's cupboard. But, Christobel Mackenzie asks, '[w]hat can this possibly have to do with the real relationships people have?'[35] That is, looking at pornography is one thing, but does it mean a total breakdown in the relationship? Or looking at other people, perhaps with desire? Hardy's fiction explores this heterosexism, which states that heterosexual couplism must be the norm, with the total devotion of each partner to the other. One is not allowed to glance at anyone else, or speak about them. Having no relationship is no good either: the individual is soon hounded by society to conform and marry. Thus, Bathsheba, when Troy's buggered off, has Boldwood on one side waiting patiently but tremulously for her signal to agree to wed him after six years, and Oak on the other side, waiting even more patiently, and threatening to leave for California. In *Desperate Remedies* the narrator's bitter comment applies to many of the later Hardy heroines (Grace with Fitzpiers, Tess with Alec, Bathsheba with Troy):

> *Of all the ingenious and cruel satires that from the beginning till now have been stuck like knives into womankind, surely there is not one so lacerating to them, and to us who love them, as the trite old fact, that the most wretched of men can, in the twinkling of an eye, find a wife ready to be more wretched still for the sake of his company.* (16. 4)

As one critic notes, while for Thomas Hardy's men the crisis may be intellectual or ethical, for Hardy's women it 'is always sexual in nature'.[36]

Creating (a) 'feminist æsthetics' means writing / rewriting language, art, culture, notions of knowledge and ontology, of identity and politics, all manner of things. For Julia Kristeva, there is no 'other place' in language, for, as Ludwig Wittgenstein said, the world we live in is a world circumscribed by language. In effect, language 'writes' the world: to go beyond it is the quest for the 'wild zone', the utterly Other Place. For Kristeva, revolution must occur *within* symbolic (that is, patriarchal) language.[37] Women's writing or art becomes a literature of absence, of negative capability, revealing by what it does not reveal, forever outside yet also inside patriarchal discourse. As the Marxist-Feminist Literature Collective write:

> *Women, who are speaking subjects but partially excluded from culture, find modes of expression which the hegemonic discourse cannot integrate. Whereas the eruptive word cannot make the culturally inaccessible accessible, it can surely speak its absence.*[38]

Julia Kristeva asks questions which are central to feminist æsthetics and 'women's' art. Will there be a visionary feminism which takes women's art (French feminists use the term 'writing' to cover cultural/ creative activities) into a new era?

> *Or is it, on the contrary and as avant-garde feminists hope, that having started with the idea of difference, feminism will be able to break free of its belief in woman, her power, her writing, so as to channel this demand for difference into each and every element of the female whole, and, finally, to bring out the singularity of each woman, and beyond this, her multiplicities, her plural languages, beyond the horizon, beyond sight, beyond faith itself?*[39]

Kristeva is very positive, though, despite her insistence on absence. She is uncompromising; in "Freud and Love" she says she believes in the 'notion of emptiness, which is at the heart of the human psyche'.[40] Yet she is optimistic, too. Her philosophy is founded on absence, yet she often writes of the possibility that a 'wild zone' or otherness has been neglected, that there maybe a nighttime space, of the unconscious, of magic or otherness. In *Women's Time* she asks more questions:

> Is it because, faced with social norms, literature reveals a certain knowledge and sometimes the truth itself about an otherwise repressed nocturnal, secret and unconscious universe? Because it thus redoubles the social contract by exposing the unsaid, the uncanny? (*The Kristeva Reader*, 207)

And, again from *Women's Time*, Kristeva argues for aspects of female subjectivity that could exist outside of patriarchy:

> As for time, female subjectivity would seem to provide a specific measure that essentially retains repetition and eternity from among the multiple modalities of time known through the history of civilizations. On the one hand, there are cycles, gestation, the eternal recurrence of a biological rhythm which conforms to that of nature and imposes a temporality whose stereotypes shock, but whose regularity and unison with what is experienced as extra-subjective time, cosmic time, occasion vertiginous visions and unnameable jouissance. On the other hand, and perhaps as a consequence, there is the massive presence of a monumental temporality, without cleavage or escape, which has so little to do with linear time (which passes) that the very word 'temporality' hardly fits: all-encompassing and infinite like imaginary space, this temporality reminds one of Kronos in Hesiod's mythology, the incestuous son whose massive presence covered all of Gaea in order to separate her from Ouranos, the father. (ib., 191)

Language is central to the creation of a 'feminist æsthetics'. Women are denied the place to really *speak*, as many feminists note. Luce Irigaray remarked:

> When a girl begins to talk, she is already unable to speak of/to herself. Being exiled in man's speech, she is already unable to auto-affect. Man's language separates her from her mother and from other women, and she speaks it without speaking in it.[41]

In *The Woodlanders*, Grace Melbury, like many other Thomas Hardy heroines, does not have men's deftness with language. The narrator says that '[s]he could not explain the subtleties of her feelings as clearly as he [her father] could state his opinion' (XXII). Firm masculine opinion or fact is set against feminine subtlety which verges on the inarticulate. The poet, in a sense, writes inside the mother, or from the mother, or from the maternal realm. 'The poet's *jouissance* that causes him to emerge from schizophrenic decorporealization is the *jouissance* of the mother' writes Kristeva (1986, 192). But why, Kristeva asks, 'is the speaking subject incapable of uttering the mother within her very self? Why is it that the "mother herself" does not exist?' And why, Kristeva adds, is the mother only phallic? (*Desire in Language*, 194).

THOMAS HARDY AND JACQUES LACAN

Biographers and critics of Thomas Hardy have long remarked upon his witnessing of two hangings. The first one occurred on August 9 1856, when the 16 year-old Hardy saw Martha Brown hanged. The sight apparently deeply impressed Hardy. The erotic component, related in the *Life* – seeing her 'tight black silk gown' accentuating her figure – was also evident, according to Hardy's biographer. 'No boy of sixteen could have escaped being affected by the ghastly juxtaposition of sex and death' (commented Martin Seymour-Smith, 33). It wasn't just sex and death that were combined, it was sex, death and *looking*. In the *Life* Hardy feels guilty for witnessing the hanging.

The intense scopophilic element was also in evidence in the other execution Hardy witnessed. While living at Bockhampton, he heard about the hanging taking place in Dorchester at eight in the morning. He went onto the heath with a brass telescope to see it. Just as he put the 'scope to his eye he saw the white figure falling.

> The whole thing had been so sudden [he writes in the *Life*], that the glass nearly fell from Hardy's hands. He seemed alone on the heath with the hanged man, and crept home wishing he had not been so curious.

It is the last sentence that speaks of the intensity of the experience – he felt alone on the heath with the hanged man, there was a sense of total identification with the victim, with the drama of the execution. After the intensity, comes the guilt at having witnessed the event; Hardy reacts like people who gleefully watch horror films then wish afterwards that they hadn't: the images of violence often persist. Somehow, Hardy realizes, by deliberately going out onto the hill to see the execution, he was implicated in it. The sight of it connects him to the victim, the gallows, the executioner, the officials and the crowd watching. Young Tom Hardy becomes a Peeping Tom. The intensity of this event is emphasized by Hardy's visual description of it: the sun behind him shining on the white gaol, with the 'murderer in white fustian' and the officials in dark clothes.

The next step biographers and critics usually make is to connect these experiences of execution to Tess's, which's witnessed from a distance. Feminist critics have noted, though, that what is specifically *not seen* is Tess's hanging, her body in its final grotesque act. Instead, the flag indicates her death. What is significant about Hardy and the executions he witnessed were that he *saw* them, and was guiltily fascinated with them. The ideology of the Lacanian gaze is very much at work in these memories related in the *Life*. One sees them not only in Tess's death, but in most of Hardy's work. As Irigaray says, women remind men of their own body, mortality and nature. Susan Griffin wrote 'a woman's body, by inspiring desire in a man, must recall him to his own body'. This is the age-old linking of women with sex and death.

In the œdipal complex, when the father enters the mother-child dyad, a series of displacements occur and the mother becomes the perpetually lost object (J. Kristeva, 1982, 62f). 'Distance from the 'origin' (the maternal)' writes Mary Ann Doane, 'is the prerequisite to desire; and insofar as desire is defined as the excess of demand over a need aligned with the maternal figure, the woman is left behind.' (1987, 173) In her essay on Hardy's early novels, Judith Wittenberg speaks of the 'voyeuristic moment' in Hardy's fiction, when the 'seeing subject and the seen object intersect in a diegetic node that both explicitly and implicitly suggests the way in which the world is constituted in and through the scopic drive.' (1983, 151)

One can see how important looking or voyeurism is in Thomas Hardy's fiction, for voyeurism is founded on keeping a spatial distance between subject and object, as Christian Metz noted.[42] Distancing encourages eroticism, because the system of representation – an image of a woman standing in for the real woman – makes the reality less threatening. And, importantly, representations of the erotic object (women) are easier to manipulate to suit one's own ends than 'real' women, as Hardy's male characters know well.[43] Hardy's lovers love from a distance, but when they behold the beloved up close, their desire withers. When the Hardy lover finally unites with the beloved, the former dissatisfaction returns. 'With contact loves dies' (J. Miller, 1970, 176). For French feminists such as Hélène Cixous, the philosophy of the Lacanian 'lack' is ridiculous. As she writes in "The Laugh of the Medusa": '[w]hat's a desire originating from a lack? A pretty meagre desire.' (E. Marks, 262) And Luce Irigaray and other feminists (Koman, Grosz, Montrelay, Doane) have criticized the Freudian-Lacanian emphasis on the phallus as the 'transcendental signifier', as the measure of authentic sexual pleasure.[44] What woman lacks is lack itself, says Montrelay, an inability to create distance and representation (Tess is denied this).

From Plato to Freud and Lacan the desire/ lack has been central to Western sexual metaphysics: in this negative model, one is doomed to a desire for more and more consumption, which leads to dissatisfaction. The 'lack' or emptiness at the heart of Hardy's lovers can only momentarily be filled. Erotic plenitude never lasts (J. Miller, 1970, 184). Freudian-Lacanian desire can never be satisfied: dissatisfaction is built-in. Desire is never annihilated: for Georg Wilhelm Hegel, only another desire can satisfy desire and also perpetuate it. Desire thus desires more desire (this has a vivid expression in late capitalist consumerism, where it is always the *next* commodity that will truly satisfy and stop the hunger for more objects. But it never happens).

Another way of looking at desire is not to see it as the (unattainable) search for satisfaction stemming from a lack (Jacques Lacan), nor as related to denial and prohibition (Sigmund Freud), but rather as a positive force of fullness and production, that creates interactions, that makes connections between things. Instead of internalization and obliteration (Hegel), desire may join and make things (Friedrich Nietzsche and Benedict Spinoza). For Gilles Deleuze and Félix Guattari (*pace*

Spinoza and Nietzsche), desire is a positive force, 'inherently full. Instead of a yearning, desire is seen as an actualization, a series of practices, action, production' (Elizabeth Grosz).45 As Hélène Cixous says: 'my desires have invented new desires' (E. Marks, 246).

The poetic moment, for Kristeva, is founded on desire: desire is what keeps the system together:

The other that will guide you and itself through this dissolution is a rhythm, music, and within language, a text. But what is the connection that holds you both together? Counter-desire, the negative of desire, inside-out desire, capable of questioning (or provoking) its own infinite quest. Romantic, filial, adolescent, exclusive, blind and Oedipal: it is all that, but for others. It returns to where you are, both of you, disappointed, irritated, ambitious, in love with history, critical, on the edge and even in the midst of its own identity crisis. (Desire in Language, 165)

On desire, Kristeva writes, in "Psychoanalysis and the Polis":

Desire, the discourse of desire, moves towards its object through a connection, by displacement and deformation. The discourse of desire becomes a discourse of delirium when it forecloses its object, which is always already marked by that 'minus factor' mentioned earlier, and when it establishes itself as the complete locus of jouissance (full and without exteriority). In other words, no other exists, no object survives in its irreducible alterity. (1986, 308)

The Lacanian Look emphasizes eroticism. Seeing is erotic, the eye becomes a kind of phallus, caressing the obscure object of desire, which it can never 'possess'. As the poet Rainer Maria Rilke wrote '[g]azing is a wonderful thing.'46 The act of looking eroticizes the object. The Look is an assertion of male power and sexuality. 'Male desire is presented as a response to female beauty' states Andrea Dworkin (Intercourse, 114). Margaret Whitford glosses Luce Irigaray's work thus:

Western systems of representation privilege seeing: what can be seen (presence) is privileged over what cannot be seen (absence) and guarantees Being, hence the privilege of the penis which is elevated to the status of the Phallus. (30)

Lacanian psychoanalysis is a hell of misrepresentations and mis-readings, mirrors and imaginary spaces. The subject in the Lacanian system is constantly trying to make good mistakes made in its early psychosexual growth. In the dreaded mirror phase, the image becomes a mirage, and a distance is set up between the image and the body, an absence which Lacan termed the *objet a*. In the confusions of the three realms, the symbolic, real and imaginary, the subject cannot realize what it most wants to realize. The objects of desire remain forever elusive.

There is something inexplicably depressing about Lacan's version of psychosexual events. Lovers, in the Lacanian system, desire what they cannot have. The problem of the lack, the *objet a* and *la chose*, can never be resolved. Lacanian philosophy posits, among other things (here we go): an eternal search for what can never be found.[47] The Freudian-Lacanian system demands a continuous series of substitutions for the objects to fill the primordial lack. It is a system of replacing an imaginary and immobile plenitude that will always fail. The primal realm remains always lost or forbidden. The Paradise of early childhood recedes ever further into the distance of the past.

In the Jungian system, Beatrice, Laura, Cleopatra, Isolde, Eurydice, Ariadne and all those women of myth, poetry and legend, are incarnations of the *anima*, which is, as Carl Jung explains, something all males possess: '[e]very man carries with him the eternal image of woman, not the image of this or that particular woman, but a definitive feminine image.'[48] The *anima* is 'a personification of the unconscious in a man, which appears as a woman or a goddess in dreams, visions and creative fantasies', write Emma Jung and Marie-Louise von Franz.[49] Male writers throughout history have depicted their version of the *anima*, it seems. Each (male) writer has a version of the 'inner feminine figure' as Jung calls her. (C. Jung, 1967, 210-1) For artists, this idealized *anima* figure seems to be another manifestation of that obscure object of desire, the eroticized woman, a mirror for male lust. The equation is: the more sublime and voluptuous the woman is depicted, the more sublime and voluptuous is the artist's desire. In Thomas Hardy's fiction, characters such as Sue, Tess and Eustacia have a powerful *anima* component for their male suitors.

Further; in Lacanian psychology, desire, which is the foundation of the system, is enmeshed with speaking, with creativity and art. The œdipal crisis and the repression of the desire for the mother occurs with the entry into the Symbolic Order, and the entry into language. As Toril Moi crystallizes Lacan's thought so concisely: '[t]o speak as a subject is therefore the same as to represent the existence of repressed desire.' (1988, 99-100) Men gaze at women and manipulate them into erotic poses (Jude with Sue, Alec and Angel with Tess, Wildeve and Clym with Eustacia, Henchard, problematically, with Elizabeth-Jane). Larysa Mykyta writes:

> *The sexual triumph of the male passes through the eye, through the contemplation of the woman. Seeing the women ensures the satisfaction of wanting to be seen, of having one's desire recognized, and thus comes back to the original aim of the scopic drive. Woman is repressed as subject and desired as object in order to efface the gaze of the Other, the gaze that would destroy the illusion of reciprocity and oneness that the process of seeing usually supports. The female object does not look, does not have its own point of view; rather it is erected as an image of the phallus sustaining male desire.*[50]

The same social and ideological forces that operate in Thomas Hardy's novels are at large in the contemporary Western world. A Lady Jayne fashions advert of the mid-1990s, for example, shows a woman and a man about to kiss, in colour and close-up, over two pages. The copy to this heterosexual, romantic (and white) ad echoes the Lacanian pleasure of looking in Hardy's fiction:

> *One look, THE look, and you know you're in for an enchanted evening. It starts with beautiful hair, irresistibly dressed with fashion accessories by Lady Jayne. It ends with a kiss... Or perhaps rather more?*[51]

The 'rather more' here means romance, a relationship, and fucking, of course. In other words, with the help of Lady Jayne hair fashions one might end up fucking someone at the end of the evening. A night which begins with 'beautiful hair' might end with 'rather more', i.e., 'heterosexual intercourse'. Throughout women's magazines (all magazines, all media), we see these bourgeois romantic scenarios at work, where, at the end of the evening, tupping is the apotheosis, the 'happy ever after' ending of fairy tales, the delicious icing on the cake, the ultimate way of 'rounding off' a night out. It's a yawn, but Cinderella myths sell products.

The most intense sequence of erotic looking in Thomas Hardy's fiction occurs in the opening of *Far From the Madding Crowd*. Here is the classic Lacanian scenario of a man looking at a woman without her knowing. The Lacanian/ filmic undercurrent is exaggerated when Bathseba Everdene takes out a mirror and looks at herself, smiling. The language depicts erotic pleasure – Bathsheba has her eyes half-closed, parts her lips and smiles, and blushes profusely. The narrator even reminds the reader of the novelty of the event taking place outdoors, instead of in a bedroom (chapter I). When Oak confronts Bathsheba, returning her hat, Hardy's narrator makes the power of phallic voyeurism explicit:

> *Rays of male vision seem to have a tickling effect upon virgin faces in rural districts; she brushed hers with her hand as if Gabriel had been irritating its pink surface by actual touch…* (III)

The intensity of Lacanian desire and Freudian projection is underlined at the end of chapter II when Gabriel Oak is described as having a lack or void inside him:

> *Having for some time known the want of a satisfactory form to fill an increasing void within him, his position moreover affording the widest scope for his fancy, he painted her a beauty.* (II)

Jude Fawley has the same lack inside him after seeing Arabella for the first time: before meeting her, he didn't know it was there. Similarly, before Gabriel meet Bathsheba, he is reasonably content. Her arrival makes him realize his life is not complete without a woman.

The pleasure of the text, whether the text is a painting, film, magazine, photograph, piece of theatre, and so on, comes, according to Roland Barthes, when the Look of the spectator is aligned with that of the author.[52] Judith Wittenberg speaks of Thomas Hardy's 'spectatorial narrator' (1983, 152). What feminist criticism has done is to question the masculine 'pleasure of the text', arguing for a feminist reading of the traditional masculine or patriarchal view of texts. This debate has been central to feminism's approach to Hardy's fiction – the problem of the gender of the narrator and spectator. 'Hardy's narrators persist in constructing and interpreting female characters according to standard notions about woman's weakness, inconstancy, and tendency to hysteria' commented Kristin Brady.[53]

For some feminists, there can be no true 'feminist gaze', because the Look is always masculine, ultimately. If the spectator is a 'gendered object', suggests Annette Kuhn, then 'masculine subjectivity [is] the only subjectivity available' (A. Kuhn, 1982, 63). The politics of representation, which are central to the consumption of culture and art, are weighted firmly in favour of men and patriarchy. As John Berger writes: 'men act and women appear'. Catherine King notes: 'most images in masculine visual ideology are created to empower men as spectators – that is, to see themselves as endlessly important with things laid out for their desire'.[54]

Post-Lacanian feminists such as Luce Irigaray argue that subjectivity can only be attributed to women with difficulty. Irigaray claims that 'any theory of the subject has always been appropriated by the 'masculine'' (*Speculum*, 133). 'Woman' is tied to a 'non-subjective subjectum' (ib., 265). Irigaray stresses the sexed being, the sexualized subject and speaking position. No form of knowledge or philosophy can be authentic or 'universal' if it ignores the 'female' position.

Irigaray concentrates on the act of enunciation, the act of producing discourse. Irigaray stresses the interiority of the speaking subject, the traces of subjectivity found in acts of communication. The continual denial of a sexualized discourse threatens the possibility of an emergent non-patriarchal society. Irigaray has investigated the use by men and women of everyday language, concluding that men and women privilege different patterns of speech, with men encouraging their 'self-affection', or relations to/ with the self and the self projecting in others, while women use language to make connections and relationships with both sexes. Irigaray's deconstruction of the languages of science, philosophy and politics has demonstrated the repression of the feminine – Dale Spender and other feminists have come to similar conclusions. For Irigaray, this repression is not in-built into language, but reflects the (patriarchal) social order. In order to change one the other must also be changed.

Luce Irigaray's argument fits in exactly to a feminist reading of Thomas Hardy's fiction, in particular of *Tess of the d'Urbervilles* as a study of the relations between speaking, language, sexuality, identity, power and patriarchy. Irigaray says that if the vagina is regarded as a 'hole', it is a 'negative' space that cannot be represented in the dominant discourse. Thus to have a vagina is to be deprived of a voice, to be decentred or culturally subordinated, and so Irigaray replaces Lacan's mirror with a vaginal speculum.[55]

One feminist critic of *Tess of the d'Urbervilles* puns Tess's 'wholeness' with her 'holeness', that is, Tess as sexual lack or vagina waiting to be filled by the male characters and the reader gendered as male by the narration.[56] The phallic privileging of the masculine 'I' (penis, phallus, power, identity, soul – Alec and Angel) means that female sexuality is rendered 'invisible', just as the vagina is a negative space or void (Tess). The phallus is the divine, beloved mirror, emblem of masculine narcissism ('"You are Eve, and I am the old Other One"' mocks Alec in chapter 50). But the vagina, being a 'black hole', can reflect back nothing. There is no self there. Male speculations and narcissistic gazes create a male subject: the mistakes arise when this male subject is equated with the whole world. This occurs in the perception of Alec and Angel, who cannot comprehend realms of sexuality and ideology outside of the phallocentric, patriarchal norms. The universality of philosophy and psychoanalysis thus becomes founded on a one-sided (male) view of the world (the narrator in Hardy's novels also ambiguously embodies this view). Male sexuality and narcissism mistakenly becomes the basis for the universal model of sexuality of psychoanalysis. Female sexuality becomes the negative image of male sexuality, if female subjectivity is considered at all (Sue Bridehead and Tess Durbeyfield continually deny their own sexual desires). Women are supposed to have 'penis envy', a hankering for the transcendent signifier which will enable them to attain a positive, creative identity. Freudian 'penis envy' has been rejected by most feminists.

One can see how Luce Irigaray would have upset Jacques Lacan, who founded his theory of sexuality, like Sigmund Freud, on the primary of the phallus. In the Freudian-Lacanian phallic system, all is unity, identity, singularity (going all the way back through history to that initial 'singularity', the Big Bang). Ambiguity, multiplicity and excess are excluded from this view: Luce Irigaray's project of rewriting Freud and Lacan disrupts the isomorphic unity and replaces it with a series of dense, poetic, parodic discourses, in which female repression is unleashed and the female unconscious is allowed to explode into academic patriarchy. Irigaray's specular project disrupts the insistence in phallic, patriarchal sexuality on one organ (penis), one orgasm or pleasure (male), one identity (male), one model of representation (masculine). Irigaray's notion of 'feminine writing' disrupts the unitary dimensions of the phallocratic system ('there would be no longer be either subject or object' Irigaray wrote of the new 'female syntax' in *This Sex Which Is Not One*, and 'oneness' would no longer be privileged' (134)).

For some feminists, Luce Irigaray's rewriting of Lacan is still as essentialist as Lacan's phallic discourse; for others, Irigaray's specular discourse is not essentialist, for 'Irigaray is nobody's fool, [and] not Lacan's'.[38] Some critics who are more sympathetic to Irigaray's thought (M. Whitford, N. Schor, J. Gallop, E. Grosz, J. Féral, C. Burke, D. Fuss) offer a more sophisticated reading than those feminist critics (T. Moi, M. Plaza, J. Sayers, A. Jones) who see nothing but essentialism in Irigaray's philosophy (C. Weedon, 1987, 63; D. Stanton, 1986, 160; M. Plaza, 1978; J. Sayers, 1986, 42; B. Brown, 1979, 38). Irigaray, though, emphasizes not so much biological as morphological feminist strategies: her emphasis is very much on forms of representation of the body, and how these modes of representation relate to society and social ethics. It is the social inscription of corporeality, not the anatomical body in itself, that is important.

Luce Irigaray writes that '[m]en always go further, exploit further, seize more, without really knowing where they are going' (*Thinking*, 5). It can't be simply a case of 'blaming' men for everything, as Simone de Beauvoir said – blame men, yes, but also blame 'the system' (society). Luce Irigaray thinks that the abstraction 'equality' can only mean *at best* the equality of salaries, so that women will be paid the same as men; nothing else, Irigaray says, can be 'equal'; instead, there must eternal *difference*, in gender, from the sexual to the cultural. Irigaray says that difference must be emphasized, but her theory of difference is based, like the metaphysics of Dworkin, on sexuality. Sexuality lies at the heart of the feminist discourse of feminists such as Dworkin, Irigaray, Hélène Cixous, Kate Millet, Susan Griffin and Shere Hite; they emphasize sexuality more than other factors, and this is a problem, this reduction, ultimately, to sexual matters. Donna C. Stanton has criticized Cixous' theories, seeing in them a return to the metaphysics of presence and identity, in which the technique of poetic metaphor suggests an economy of similitude, instead of one of difference (D. Stanton, 1986).

Irigaray's views on 'gender equality' revolve around notions of women's sexual difference:

> The demand to be equal presupposes a point of comparison. To whom or to what do women want to be equalized? To men? To a salary? to a public office? To what standard? Why not to themselves? (1993, 12)

For Irigaray, the exploitation of women derives from sexual difference, so the solution, she says, 'will only come through sexual difference' (1993, 12). Women's oppression and exploitation, says Irigaray, is incredible, bearing in mind where men come from.

> We still live in a framework of familio-religious relations in which the woman is the body to the man's head. It's quite astonishing that men, whom in their cradle were totally dependent upon women in who owe their existence to this dependence, should then take the liberty of turning things around: men exist thanks to women's intelligence, but apparently women aren't capable of governing society or even of being full citizens... In an incredibly distrustful manœuvre, it's suspected that they would no longer want to protect life the moment they themselves have a right to it. women are often nothing more than hostages of the reproduction of the species. (1993, 78)

Though fervent was our vow,
Though ruddily ran our pleasure,
Bliss has fulfilled its measure,
    And sees its sentence now.

Ache deep, but make no moans:
Smile out; but stilly suffer:
The paths of love are rougher
    Than thoroughfares of stones.

Thomas Hardy, 'The End of the Episode' (CP, 227)

Early on in his writing career, at the time of *The Poor Man and the Lady*, Thomas Hardy recognized the importance of erotic desire in fiction: 'as a rule no fiction will considerably interest readers rich or poor unless the passion of love forms a prominent feature in the thread of the story'.[58] Hardy's characters yearn so painfully – Eustacia Vye cries out for a great love to help her escape. 'To be loved to madness – such was her great desire' (121). Love – the great yearning – proves to be her downfall. She dies for love, like Cathy Earnshaw in *Wuthering Heights*. Hardy's women yearn, but rarely do they get an earthlover like Heathcliff. Intense love means intense death. Love now but die later – this is the Romantic credo. The love between Clym Yeobright and his mother is equally intense, and destructive. It reaches a profundity of painfulness (VI. i). Tess Durbeyfield lives, for a season, in 'spiritual altitudes' which are ecstatic (XXXI). Her tragedy is also Eustacia Vye's and Marty South's – her yearning for love is not reciprocated. Love is not returned, passion burns itself away and is thrust out from the soul into the darkness of the universe. The self is ultimately alone – the modernist post-Romantic stance.

The narrator of *Jude the Obscure* (and also Phillotson) sees Sue and Jude as two halves of one whole – a Gnostic love-union of selves (*Jude*, IV. iv), which's called the *syzygy* in Gnosticism. In fact, their togetherness is very shaky. The dialectic of their love is continually shifting – from desire to disgust, and all the shades in between. There is no easy, simple dualism of reciprocation for Hardy. Sue and Jude drift apart and come back together in waves. They fuse then fragment, like particles in some sub-atomic experiment. It is a bout of Empodeclean Love and Strife for them, a state of Heraclitean flux, a Hegelian neurotic tension, with the world-weary detachment of Arthur Schopenhauer added.

In Sue and Jude the big themes – the pagan and the Christian, the traditional and the modern, the spiritual and the sexual – are at war. Thomas Hardy depicts love-in-flux, always being modulated, changed, destroyed, rebuilt, transfigured. Sue and Jude fly together involuntarily – such as in their kiss on the silent road, when they 'kissed close and long' (IV. iii). But soon they fall apart again. The pattern was laid down long ago in figures of myth such as Isis and Osiris, Ishtar and Tammuz, Anna and Baal, and in the later figures such as Anthony and Cleopatra, Héloïse and Abélard, and Petrarch and Laura. Hardy's narrators are heretical about love. They do not believe in marriage. Their ideas on love have much in common with the mediæval cults and heresies: of courtly love, the Cathars, Templars, Sufism, Albigensian heresy, alchemy and the cults of the Grail and the Black Virgin. Though it is not as strident as in some writers, there is in Hardy's fiction the urge towards spiritual sublimation, the transcendence of the flesh and the mysticization of the erotic.

Love in Mr Hardy's world is about two people trying to 'follow their bliss' (Joseph Campbell's term). In Hardy's novels the urge of the lovers is to escape, to find, like Sue and Jude, Angel and Tess, their own niche in the world, away from other, interferring people. Hardy put it utterly plainly and so passionately in his poem 'The Recalcitrants':

> Let us off and search, and find a place,
> Where yours and mine can be natural lives,
> Where no one comes, who dissects and dives
> And proclaims that ours is a curious case,
> Which its touch of romance can scarcely grace.
> (Complete Poems, 389)

This is the great dream of lovers – to re-create the world and to find a place in which to really live and breathe. The problem is that society and all kinds of other factors subvert this lust for loneliness. 'Love is the burning-point of life' says Joseph Campbell (Power, 205) and the tragedy of Hardy's novels, as D.H. Lawrence notes in *Study of Thomas Hardy*, is that the pioneers in love die in the wilderness (21).

Escape, but die. Remain, and live. The Kierkegaardian risk-taking is everything. Without risk there is no life. Life is lived on the edge. This risk-taking for the glory of love is the main theme in Thomas Hardy's fiction. The way he deals with it makes him 'great' – as with Fyodor Dostoievsky or William Shakespeare or Sappho. 'His feeling, his instinct, his sensuous understanding is, however, apart from his metaphysic, very great and deep, deeper than that perhaps of any other English novelist' remarked Lawrence (*Study of Thomas Hardy*, 93)

Thomas Hardy's fiction is full of supernatural sensibilities. He conversed many times with his dead wife, Emma: '[w]ould that I lay there | And she were housed here! | Or better, together | Were folded away there | Exposed to one weather | We both…' ('Rain on a Grave', CP, 441). The Hardy-poet yearns to be united with his decayed lovers, in the Emily Brontëan manner: '[t]he eternal tie which binds us twain in one | No eye will see | Stretching across the miles that sever you from me.' (CP, 421) The romantic idea of lovers meeting over distances, or at night, in dreams, or after death, extends the Western notion of the soul to its logical extreme. One aim of the writer is to make writing like love – to write and love, to make the act of writing love itself, to make desire concrete in art, the two fusing, love and art, into one life. The aim is to fuse life and love and art. As Hardy wrote in his poetry: '[l]ove lures life on.' ('Lines', in CP, 458).

One of Sappho's short lyrics on love reads:

It brings us pain
and weaves myths.[39]

This describes concisely the dominant discourse of love in Thomas Hardy's (and most) fiction: the Nietzschean/ Christian emphasis on suffering, and the subsequent myth-making. (Sappho is quoted in *Jude the Obscure*, though with a different meaning – referring to Sue in the epigram to 'Part Third, 'At Melchester').

Love in Hardy's work is Keatsian and Shelleyan. Hardy's work is fleshly, sensuous but also doomed. His love-affairs take much of their flavour from poems such as John Keats' 'La Belle Dame Sans Merci'. Elfride, in her vanity, asks Stephen from her pony in *A Pair of Blue Eyes*: '"Do I seem like La belle dame sans merci?"' (57). The reference probably suggested itself to Hardy as he constructed this scene. The fairy queen/knightly lover motifs feature also in the romances of Bathsheba and Oak, Sue and Jude, Eustacia and Clym. The dark sensualism of Keats is well suited to Hardy's work. Hardy is a slave to love, as a poet, as he is a slave to women, to Woman, like poets such as Dante Alighieri, Francesco Petrarch, John Donne, Robert Herrick and Robert Graves. Hardy's women are Muses who throw down enchantments over the initiate's soul and senses. Hardy's beloveds are the Symbolist and Decadent Fatal Women, the pale wraiths eulogized by poets such as Charles Baudelaire, A.C. Swinburne and Samuel Taylor Coleridge, and by Franz von Stuck. Gustave Moreau and Félicien Rops in painting. Robert Graves had his Laura Riding, as Hardy had his Emma Gifford. The poetry records a haunting of the poet-alone by the Elf-Queen. The antecedents of this scenario are many – the classic one in English literature being of course Shakespeare and his formidable Dark Lady, she '[w]ho art as black as hell, as dark as night' (last line of sonnet no. 147).

Another ancestor is Merlin's enthrallment at the hands of Ninue. In the poesie of John Keats and Percy Bysshe Shelley and the Elizabethan poets we find the powerful spirit of Arthuriana, embodied in figures such as the Lady of Shalott or Morgan Le Fey, before they became trivialized in late Victorian poetry and Pre-Raphaelitism. These romantic ideas surged throughout Europe in the late 12th century and afterwards with the troubadours. But England was late in incorporating Arthurian legend. The new concepts and *mœurs* of love and individualism took hold in the Elizabethans. In Thomas Campion's exaltation of the 'fairy queen Prosperina' for instance. Nothing new about these sorcerous Madonnas, however. Giraut de Borneil, Arnaut Daniel, Bernard de Ventadour and the other troubadours, *jongleurs* and minstrels had all done it before, and so well, too. William Shakespeare is the apotheosis in English literature of this kind of love-poetry. Romanticism is the end of it all – though a wild, chaotic and intense kind of death.

Thomas Hardy arrives at the very tail-end of this extended demise. What is raised up in his love-poetry is the authenticity of his experience and poetic voice. Hardy is not as violent, nor as high-flown, as the Elizabethans. Nicholas Breton wrote in *The Passionate Shepherd*: 'to kill love's maladies, | Meet her with your melodies' (in G. Hiller, 244). This is the answer – when stabbed to death by love, re-birth yourself in art, in love-poetry. Or as Keats would have it:

> *...if thy mistress some rich anger shows*
> *Emprison her soft hand, and let her rave,*
> *And feed deep, deep upon her peerless eyes*[60]

Hardy's poetic persona is not as assertive as Keats or Shakespeare, though there is still the same masochistic misogyny in some of his poetry. The Hardyan lover though, like Shakespeare, wants to be slain by his beloved. 'Kill me outright with looks', implores the Shakespearean poet, while Jude, at the terrible climax of his romance with Sue, also implores his black Mistress:

> "Don't go – don't go!... This is my last time! I... shall never come again. Don't then be unmerciful, Sue, Sue! we are acting by the letter, and the letter killeth!" (Jude the Obscure, VI. viii)

The letter, the vicious law of a dying religion, Christianity, certainly does kill. So the poet begs for *merci*, that key blessing in Renaissance and chivalric love-poetry. But the poet knows it is useless – it is all over, just as Tess cries, but hopelessly '"Have Mercy!"' (XXXV) The romances of Jude-Sue have a Shelleyan subtext to them. They are built upon an ætherealizing orientation of spirit-over-sex. Shelley's poem 'When Passion's Trance is Overpast' forms the philosophical basis of Hardy's romances:

> *If it were enough to feel, to see*
> *Thy soft eyes gazing tenderly,*
> *And dream the rest – and burn and be*
> *The secret food of fires unseen,*
> *Could thou but be what thou hast been.*[62]

Love without touching, sex through spirituality, a deeply sensuous love-act transcending skin and ordinary sense – this is a common ambition in Hardyan Wessexuality. Think of all those poems of Thomas Hardy's, in which the poet meets some beloved by night, but they do not touch or kiss, just talk. Hardy aims to spiritualize love, but in a heterodox, not doctrinal, manner. *Jude the Obscure* records the failure of this sacralization of love, its near-impossible fusion with everyday domestic and economic life. Hardy's holy love, like Shelley's, needs a sacred, secret place away from other people, in which to flourish. But there's none left. So you have to create your own – and how difficult that is. Hardy's lovers aim to do this: '[l]et us off and search, and find a place' Hardy wrote in 'The Recalcitrants'. But they fail. Robert Herrick wrote the same pæan: '[c]ome, let us go while we are in our prime' (in 'Corrinna's Going-a-Maying'). It is an anti-social ambition, an escapism in love almost wholly unrealizable.

Thomas Hardy is very bitter about this secular failure to recapture an earlier hermetic love-time. In his poem 'She to Him i' he wrote: '[t]hat Sportsman Time but rears his brood to kill' (CP, 15). This is the bleak view of Tess, who wishes she'd never been born into this cynical game of the gods. Hardy tries to look honestly and clearly at life – to go after the 'offensive truth' (Per, 26). His pessimism is really 'evolutionary meliorism' (ib, 52). As he says in the poem 'In Tenebris': 'if a Better way there be, it exacts a full look at the Worst' (CP, 168). Hardy depicts people full of 'fret and fever' (Per, 42), the idea is 'given the man and woman, how to find a basis for their sexual relation' (ib, 19). Hardy quotes his beloved Shakespeare in support of his claims: 'life [is] time's fool' (Per, 47, quoting *King Henry* iv i, V, iv, 81). The flipside is '[l]ove's not Time's fool' (sonnet no. 116).

The work of Shakespeare and Hardy is the result of the attempt to fuse these two viewpoints – the hopeless and the idealistic. Love's not time's fool, but life is – how typically of two realist and often determinist artists to be so ambivalent. They know love and life and art and time and death cannot be simply reconciled. In both Hardy and Shakespeare Time marches on, unstoppable, even though, sometimes, it 'must have a stop'. No. It eats everything away, demolishing all as it sweeps by. Wes-sex-mania ends up as a drowned body in a heathland river (*The Return of the Native*), or a hanged woman in Winchester goal (*Tess of the d'Urbervilles*), or a derelict dying in Oxford (*Jude the Obscure*), or a corpse in a Dorset wood (*The Woodlanders*).

How desolate Thomas Hardy's view of the outcome of love seems to be. He is an optimist blasted by life's shocks into bitter realism. His works record satires of circumstance, life's little ironies and time's laughingstocks, those human shows with their few moments of vision, offensive truths hidden amongst post-pastoral Wessex tales.

How forlorn Thomas Hardy actually is can be adjudged from the endings to his tragic novels, and throughout his poetry. Tragedies must end in death, it seems (but how awful and ludicrous is Viviette's collapse at the end of *Two on a Tower*). There is much doom and gloom in the poetry. It is there in the early poems – in 'Neutral Tones', for example. Hardy's imagery in this short lyric is bleak, while the poem's sparseness looks forward to Samuel Beckett: the white sun, dead pond, barren earth (these are stage-settings for *Waiting For Godot* or *Happy Days*). Hardy rages here, too, though in a quiet way – the poet learns that 'love deceives' and thus the sun, the innocent, utterly non-human sun, becomes 'God-curst' (CP, 12). This is typical of the love-poem in the West: the jilted lover must have the outside world reflect his/ her desolation.

The futile scene in 'Neutral Tones' is picked up in Thomas Hardy's last novel – it forms the opening of *Jude the Obscure*. Jude, the 'natural boy', works in the 'wide and lonely depression of the empty field' (I. iii). The depth of Hardy's rage is clear from the way he develops this scene – Jude soon gets beaten up by Farmer Troughton, and whirled around like a toy. The target of Hardy's anger is made explicit – it is not God, nor the birds nor nature, but the human world in which Jude lives (I. iii).

Thomas Hardy is bitterly ironic in his use of Percy Shelley as one of the major discourses in *Jude the Obscure*. Hardy counters his grim realism with a Shelleyan aching for sweetness and release. It is this quivering yearning that powers Eustacia Vye, Tess Durbeyfield, Sue Bridehead and Jude Fawley, and also Pierston in *The Well-Beloved* in his Platonic search for a Shelleyan 'Beloved'. Eustacia, Tess and Sue are Shelleyan heroines, yearning for a delicacy of touch and spirit that the workaday world simply cannot provide. The gulfs between the two form the tension at the heart of the Hardy novel (*Life*, 272). These conflicts force the Hardyan anti-hero to cry, with Shelley: 'O World, o Life, o Time'.

Thomas Hardy can be seen as ultimately an optimist. He does weave in an escape-clause at the end of his novels, most prophetically (and ambiguously) in the figures of Angel and Tess's sister, as a New Adam and Eve. And in 'The Darkling Thrush', with its heartfelt synthesis of the poetry of Keats, Shelley and Wordsworth, Hardy rejoices that out of the waste land a bird can still sing, and that 'there trembled through/ His happy good-night air/ Some blessed Hope' (CP, 150).

The Promethean rebellion in Thomas Hardy's fiction occurs in sexual politics and erotic desire. For Hardy's disaffected, dispossessed, depressed and often displaced characters, the way out is through/ by / in/ with love. In Hardy's fictive world, religion no longer offers moments of ecstasy and union, but love, the 'profane' experience, still does. What Jude does is what all Hardy's lovers do: he creates a religion of love around Sue, what Stendhal called the 'crystallization of love'.[62] The problems arise because there is a gulf between the individual's wishes and what society demands of the individual. What Jude does is to build up a cult or religious aura around Sue, and the more it's built up, the greater his fall will be. Aunt Druisilla recognizes the danger of such erotic objectification and warns Jude against it. Jude has to realize, and it's painful, that Sue Bridehead will not conform to his psychic projection of her as a virginal essence. In the Godless world of Hardy's lovers, the beloved has to stand in for divinity, much as the lady of courtly love poetry was a divinity akin to the Virgin Mary. However, no individual can replace God or divinity, and the result is always disillusion for Hardy's lovers.

American Jungian Joseph Campbell wrote of marriage:

There are two stages [of marriage]. *First is what I call the biological stage which has to do with producing and raising children, and the other is what I would the alchemical marriage – realizing the spiritual identity that the two are somehow one person. It is the image of the androgyne, the male/ female being. That is the image of what is being realized through a marriage. In that mythological reference the two are one. (This business,*

22)

Hardy's couples rarely even get to the physical/ sexual/ parental stage, let alone the spiritual/ alchemical stage. Often they are in a rush to be spiritually fused, and ignore everything else. They trip up. The sexual/ domestic level is so problematic that the spiritual/ emotional side has no hope of working out successfully. In Thomas Hardy's world of love, the two-in-oneness is continually scuppered by the demands of sexuality, materialism, economics, politics and society. In Hardy's fiction, 'weddings be funerals', as Widow Edlin put it in *Jude the Obscure*. Marriage is called we*dlock*: Arabella brandishes the 'padlock' of wedlock (her wedding ring) to her neighbours in her second marriage with Jude. It's usual for tragedies to end with death, while romances, fairy tales and comedies climax with marriage. In Hardy's fiction, tragedies often begin with marriage, while the 'pastoral' or 'romance' novels always contain marriage. Interestingly, Hardy described Tess's condition in the latter part of the narrative as being a living death: for Hardy, Tess is a 'mere corpse drifting with a current to her end' (E. Blunden, 1942). A curious way to regard one's favourite heroine, but typically Hardyan.

The alchemical 'two-in-oneness' is most powerfully evoked in *Jude the Obscure*, but it occurs throughout his work, as throughout Western culture. There is always the hope that, somewhere, somehow, at some time, a sexual love can be united with a spiritual love. It is this desire for a unity of sex and spirit as well as two lovers, that lies behind *Romeo and Juliet*, Dante Alighieri's *Vita Nuova*, Petrarch's *Canzoniere*, John Donne's *Songs and Sonnets* and Emily Brontë's *Wuthering Heights*. Thomas Hardy's lovers believe, against all the odds, in the spiritualization of love. They know the sexualization of love, this is what provides the stories with much of their dramatic tension. Love exists in a nostalgic past or in a never-to-be-attained future. 'The *meeting*, then, mixing pleasure and promise or hopes, remains in a sort of future perfect' writes Julia Kristeva.[63]

The relation between love and language for Kristeva pivots around primary narcissism:

...when one transposes into language the idealization on the edge of primal repression that amatory experience amounts to, this assumes that scription and writer invest in language in the first place precisely because it is a favourite object – a place for excess and absurdity, ecstasy and death. Putting love into words... necessarily summons up not the narcissistic parry *but what appears to me as narcissistic* economy. (*Tales of Love*, 267-8)

Writing of love perpetuates the 'narcissistic economy'.[64]

To explore her psychoanalytic theory of love, Kristeva often employs the tactic of setting things against each other, of opposites. Thus, she explores the realm of the obverse of love – hate. This is another reason, perhaps, why Hardy turned from novels to poetry, because poetry may be closer to his idea of turning writing into love. Making writing *of* the (love) experience the experience itself. This idea has a correspondence with the French feminists, with Hélène Cixous and Luce Irigaray, who speak of the *jouissance* of writing, of the sexuality of the text. Hélène Cixous speaks of literary texts which deal with 'libidinal education'. Cixous' description of these works corresponds to Hardy's *Tess of the d'Urbervilles, Jude the Obscure, The Return of the Native, The Mayor of Casterbridge* and many others:

We have worked on a group of texts which belong to what can be called the literature of apprenticeship, the **Bildungsroman***, and all of the texts – and there are a lot of them because literature is after all their domain – which relate the development of an individual, their story, the story of their soul, the story of their discovery of the world, of its joys and its prohibitions, its joys and its laws, always on the trail of the first story of all human stories, the story of* Eve and the Apple. *World literature abounds in texts of libidinal education, because every writer, every artist, is brought at one moment or another to work on the genesis of his/ her own artistic being. It is the supreme text, the one written through a turning back to the place where one plays to win or lose life.*[65]

On one level, artistic creation counters Lacanian lack and Kristevan absence: the act of writing staves off emptiness and loneliness by filling up the psychic space. As Julia Kristeva wrote in *Freud and Love: Treatment and Its Discontents*:

If narcissism is a defence against the emptiness of separation, then the whole contrivance of imagery, representations, identifications and pro-jections that accompany it on the way towards strengthening the Ego and the Subject is a means of exorcising that emptiness. (1987, 42)

At the same time, the author's characters can provide much amusement, even a kind of spiritual solace.

Thomas Hardy's novels are explorations of love and its relation to identity, self, soul, politics, class, gender, and so on. Hardy's characters try to discover the inside of the people they love. But the beloved other always remains a mystery. The mystery, however, does not prevent the intense yearning. Mystery only aggravates desire.

The mystery is that I do not understand the beings that I love the most [writes Hélène Cixous], *and that even so that does not prevent me from either loving them or understanding them: what I do not understand is their own mystery, which not even they themselves reach. But I know their incomprehensibility well.*[66]

The trouble is, in getting close to another person, all manner of social and psychological problems arise. Or as Hélène Cixous puts it: '[t]here is an apple, and straight away there is the law.' (1994, 133) With the apple comes the law: Eve (women) is punished, Cixous says, because she has access to the inside, to pleasure, to touching. Eve

is punished since she has access to pleasure, of course a positive relationship to the inside is something which threatens society and which must be controlled. That is where the series of "you-shall-not-enter" begins. (1994, 134)

In *Jude the Obscure* it is 'woman's nature' which 'breaks' up Sue and the Sue-Jude relationship – Jude is not ruined by 'man's nature' because 'man's nature' is 'a term and concept that had no currency in the nineteenth century.'[67]

Thomas Hardy's novels so graphically explore the desire and the prohibition, the lust for life and the laws that come down like walls of steel around the soul.[68] We see this agony of desire and fear so clearly in books such as *Jude the Obscure* and *The Mayor of Casterbridge*, where the apple of temptation is dangled before the protagonists, then the problems begin. At the end of *Two on a Tower* the apple of life is brutally torn away from Swithin's grasp as Viviette dies in his arms. So close, yet so far away: so much presence, and yet the agony of absence. Hélène Cixous writes:

> *It is the struggle between presence and absence, between an undesirable, unverifiable, indecisive absence, and a presence, a presence which is not only a presence: the apple is visible and it can be held up to the mouth, it is full, it has an* inside. (ib., 133)

Tess Durbeyfield is of course the character most obviously likened to Eve. And Tess finds out that the punishment is brutal for those who eat the apple. As soon as the apple appears, the prohibitions appear, the long list of 'thou shalt nots', as Sue Bridehead bitterly knows. Pleasure, in Hardy's world, as in the Christian West, is punished.

> *"Domestic laws should be made according to temperaments, which should be classified. If people are at all peculiar in character they have to suffer from the very rules that produce comfort in others!"'* (233)

Part of the problem in Hardy's fictive world of desire is that only one particular person will do. In *Sebastian*, Lawrence Durrell writes:

> *Every girl's a one-man girl, and every man too. Hence the trouble, for just anybody won't do – it's gotta be the him and the her of the fairy tale.*[69]

Thomas Hardy's lovers won't have anybody else except The One in their sights. All their desire is aimed at one person, and an alternative person won't do. For Jude it must be Sue, for Tess it must be Angel, for Marty it must be Giles, and so on. As American filmmaker Bette Gordon observed, '[u]sually the object of your obsession is less important than the fact of being obsessed.' It's the obsession that counts.[70]

If there were a magic formula or potion to make someone love you, the Hardyan lover would do anything to buy it. In fact, Vibert the quack doctor in *Jude* does sell a love potion, but it is not of course the Grail.

Hardy's lovers live on the edge. They are artists of desperation. Desire in Hardy's fiction creates dishonesty: the greater the desire, the more willing the protagonist is to achieve their desire. As John Kucich puts it, 'dishonesty is simply one of the desperate remedies of desire'.[71] The deeper the desire, the greater the risks, and potential rewards. Characters in love become increasingly desperate. Desire entraps the protagonist (often they don't recognize their entrapment), and also produces a desire to entrap other people, especially other lovers.

In *The Woodlanders* Fitzpiers tells Giles, concerning Grace Melbury, that he is in love with '"something in my own head, and no thing-in-itself outside it at all"' (XVI). In Jungian terms, Hardy's male characters have to learn how to integrate the 'feminine' side of themselves, how to discern between the *anima* and the projection of their desires and needs onto other people. Hardy's male protagonists have to assimilate the feminine, a process which is problematical and painful. Henchard, Angel, Jude and Giles find it a real struggle to identify with and assimilate the feminine.

Joseph Campbell writes:

> *The problem of therapy is to bring the "head" into harmony with the energies that are informing the body, so the transcendent energies can come though. Only when this occurs are you transparent to transcendence. This implies yielding yourself to nature; putting yourself in accord with nature and, I would say, that is the main aim of most of the mythologies of the world.* (This business, 25)

This is another way of putting the basic problem in Hardy's novels, which D.H. Lawrence called the problem of 'coming into being'. Hardy's people are not 'transparent to transcendence', rather, they are earthbound, and continually concentrate on a symbol instead of seeing through it. They are supremely literal. Like children, they have to have results *now*, and physically in front of them. Think of Grace and Giles, or Sue and Jude, or Tess and Angel, how childish they are, how they cling onto a literal interpretation of events. Joseph Campbell writes of the *Bible*, which forms such a large part of the literary-cultural background of Hardy's fiction:

> *...the Bible is a compendium of all the mistakes that have ever been made in the translation of symbolic forms into historical forms.* (ib., 44)

What Campbell means is that people mistake the 'mask' of God for God himself. They think the *Bible* is 'literal', that the miracles really happened. They miss the metaphoric nature of religion. Thomas Hardy's lovers are the same: they mistake the symbol for the thing itself. Desperate, Hardy's lovers grasp at any sign and analyze it, turning it into something much more than it is. Eustacia, stuck on Edgon Heath, grasps at anything that might enable her to escape. Hardy's lovers do not recognize the metaphoric aspect of spiritual love. For them, love must have a physical, literal, conscious manifestation. Critics do the same: they read Hardy's fiction literally, seeing in his novels a series of literal events.

The problem of being transparent or opaque to transcendence is at its most acute in *Jude the Obscure*, where the lovers fight to have their kind of supra-sexual, proto-spiritual love accepted by society. They fail, partly because society (in this case the neighbours in Oxford/ Christminster) cannot see that love between a man and woman who appear to be married does not have to be sexual. It is the very appearance of a non-sexual bond, one that, further, has not been sanctified by society and law and the church, that incenses Sue and Jude's neighbours. William Greenslade suggests that Sue and Jude could refute biological determinism and 'make their own sexuality the medium of self-definition: the text might then utter what it suppresses but continually intimates' (181).

Sue and Jude try to explore an area where heterosexuality, let alone sexuality, is not 'compulsory'. As feminists have noted, not only is heterosexuality socially and ideologically 'compulsory', in Adrienne Rich's phrase, but sexuality is compulsory: everyone is expected to be sexual, to be sexually active.[72] 'Women are expected to be in, or to want to be in, a sexual relationship'.[73] You see this so clearly with Tess Durbeyfield: Tess's mother is but the first of many people who expects Tess to desire a sexual relationship. Witness Alec's astonishment when she rejects him: *what?* he implies, *you don't desire me?* But not just women: everyone is expected to be sexual.

In the radical feminist terminology of Andrea Dworkin, Susan Griffin, Kate Millett and others, being 'sexual' is equated with being fucked. In the patriarchal system, in the view of some feminists, women cannot win: they are condemned if they don't want or have sex, but women who express their sexuality are regarded with suspicion. As adolescents, what is seen as 'natural' for boys to express, sexually, is criminal for girls. Women who admit to liking sex are 'somehow seen as 'dirty' or 'bad'; this happens to Hardy's female characters: '[w]e are so afraid to be seen as 'whores' that we accept the idea of ourselves as 'victims' if we have sex. All this does for women is make being a victim seem natural' remarked Becky Rosa.[74] Alec calls Tess Durbeyfield a whore in order to justify his seduction of her. Being seen as a 'victim' limits women, and may render them 'inert by self-pity'.[75] Being a prostitute may be the only way in which women are allowed to express themselves sexually in a fiercely patriarchal society. Thus, Alec calls Tess a whore to align himself with patriarchal culture. Christianity divides women into two basic sexual types: the Virgin Mary, the saintly, worshipped Mother, or Mary Magdalene, the whore. Tess may be seen as a latter-day form of the ancient 'holy whore', the sacred prostitutes who served Goddesses such as Cybele and Isis. What's clear is that Tess is not allowed to be both, mother and sexually active woman.

No one, in life or art, it seems, can escape from being defined by their sexual identity and activity. Thus, everyone is branded socially by what they do sexually: so, old people are defined by their sexual *in*activity and jokes are made about the non-performance of their genitals. In the media, in magazines and TV programmes, in films and radio shows, people are depicted either in or not in a sexual relationship, and the sexual relationship takes precedence over all others, over friendship, over being a child or a parent, over business and social relationships. Everyone is expected to be in, or to want to be in, a sexual relationship, and when someone isn't interested, the media hounds them, by making fun of them, by lampooning the individual's non-sexual status. One sees this so clearly in Thomas Hardy's fiction, which is all about the struggle to solve, as he puts it in *The Woodlanders*, 'the immortal puzzle – given the man and woman, how to find a basis for their sexual relation' (39). Hardy said that he felt 'very strongly that the position of man and woman in nature may be taken up and treated frankly' (E. Blunden, 1942).

Thomas Hardy is as obsessed with sex as any other novelist, but that's only because his texts reflect his socio-cultural environment; because the Western world, from the Renaissance onwards (some would say from

Classic Greek times onwards, or earlier), is obsessed with sexuality. Sex is the norm; anything outside of that is regarded suspiciously. Sue and Jude, and Tess, Grace and Anne Garland, are pursued for being non-sexual exactly as modern day celebrities who don't seem particularly interested in rutting away are regarded as abnormal by the media. It's the time when questions such as this are asked: *what, you haven't got a lover/ car/ house/ phone/ fax/ computer/ video [insert item as applicable]?* Hardy shows how society polices itself, how it constructs its sexual norms. Hardy would undoubtedly have ventured into gay and lesbian politics, had he been writing in the early 21st century (one wonders how much Hardy would have been sympathetic to, for instance, lesbian feminism, with its talk of femme tops, butch bottoms, femmes butched out, cross-dressing, butch fags in drag, butches 'femmed-out in drag', dildoes, lesbian porn, S/M porn, transvetism, camp and gender-fucking).[76]

The non-sexual activity of the modern celebrity arouses suspicion then often vindictive hassling: the tabloid press ask is s/he gay? perverted? impotent? and so on. As for the idea of friendship, holding hands, dancing, sleeping together, being together, all of this means a sexual relationship is going on: in the media and society, holding hands or doing the things that romantic, sexual couples do is not allowed unless one *is* a romantic, sexual couple.[77] In Hardy's novels, if two people hold hands, it is assumed they are in a sexual relationship. Time after time characters hold hands without being in a sexual relationship, then someone sees them. They colour up, they blush, they realize that their every gesture displays to the world their sexual identity. Sometimes it seems that to be sexual at all can be seen as a subversive act, especially outside the 'nuclear family', as American filmmaker Karin Kay noted.[78]

Thomas Hardy's women often faint, collapse, blush, go into a fever, all because of love. So important is love to Hardy's characters, that when love's course goes awry, his characters (especially the women) faint, weep or wither away. They literally die for love. And women, being the 'weaker sex', show more signs of decay than men. Hardy's narrators set out to challenge the norms of gender identity, where women are the 'weaker vessel', lapsing into hysteria, but end up submitting to the patriarchal codes.[79] Unable to describe the response to love internally,

Hardy's narrators resort, in women, to extraordinary blushes, palpitations, shiverings, sobs and falls. It is one of the most annoying aspects of Hardy's fiction, these sudden blushes or collapses. For example, when Owen recognizes Anne Seaway to be an impostor in *Desperate Remedies*, she colours up like a rainbow: her skin goes ashen grey while her pink cheeks turn purple (18. 1). The insistence on lovers reacting instantly and physically to situations is ridiculous. It is a failure of Hardy's narrators that they can't get inside the characters, but have to show their suffering on the outside. Hardy's women are like painters' canvases or movie screens in this respect, instantly displaying their emotions via uncontrollable tremblings and blushings.

Nature – sexuality, rather – is cruel in Thomas Hardy's fiction. It bypasses delicate education and civilization and careful make-up jobs, erupting in (women's) bodies uncontrollably, showing how they feel, though they might prefer to hide their emotions. Some of Hardy's women react violently to emotional shocks, as if they can't handle them: Viviette shrieks and dies in Swithin's arms in *Two on a Tower*; Miss Aldclyffe bursts a blood vessel and dies after her son's suicide in *Desperate Remedies*; Cytherea, like Grace, falls ill when it's uncertain about her marital status, and so on.

Underpinning part of *Jude the Obscure* is a utopian vision of a new relation between the sexes. Even the relatively staid Phillotson suggests that single parenthood may be preferrable to the traditional nuclear family: '"I don't see why the woman and the children should not be the unit without the man"'. Gillingham responds: '"[b]y the Lord Harry! – Matriarchy!"' (IV. iv) In their lives Sue and Jude are groping towards such a state, although Sue defers to Jude many times, as when she indulges him in his Christminster dream at the Remembrance Day celebrations, even when she knows how destructive it could be. Hardy's text does not go as far as feminist separatism, though, which some feminists, often lesbian feminists, see as 'the centre, the beating heart, the essence'.[80] In lesbian and radical feminist separatism, women keep themselves not only physically but culturally and psychologically apart from men.[81]

Thomas Hardy did not go as far as advocating such an all-female or 'matriarchal' zone, but one can see how sympathetic Hardy was to feminism, and how he would probably embrace if not radical lesbian separatism, then at least the feminist emphasis on *différance* (*pace* Jacques Derrida, Luce Irigaray, Monique Wittig). The search of Sue and Jude for a cultural place where they can love according to rules they have written themselves accords with the quest in radical lesbianism for an extra-patriarchal space. Much of *Jude the Obscure* is about being 'different' – not biologically or sexually, but socially and culturally. Monique Wittig says that the lesbian is crucial because '[l]esbian is the only concept that I know of which is beyond the categories of sex (man and woman)'.[82] Hardy would probably feel sympathetic to the lesbian and feminist quests for a new kind of socio-sexual identity. The difference is that Hardy posits his opposing discourses (Sue and Jude versus society) wholly within patriarchal culture, while radical lesbian feminism aims to go beyond patriarchy. The lesbian may exist outside of traditional heterosexual discourse, but Sue and Jude do not step beyond it. Sue and Jude are locked into two-term masculine logic, where only 'man' or 'woman' exist. All the characters in *Jude the Obscure* adhere to patriarchal constructions, from Gillingham and Phillotson, to Widow Edlin, Arabella, the people of Christminster and the colleges.

The terrible truth for lovers to learn in Thomas Hardy's fiction is that what one loves most can destroy you. The deeper they sink into love, the worse it gets for Hardy's lovers. Yet even when they are treated appallingly by their beloveds, Hardy's lovers love them even more. They 'desperately apotheosise those who reject their love',[83] they dig their own emotional graves, they hurt even more and wallow in it. Hardy's lovers embrace their own destruction.

All of Thomas Hardy's lovers dream of a total, all-consuming, and lasting love between two adults. This is part of the sovereignty of 'compulsory heterosexuality', as Adrienne Rich calls it. In her essay on *Romeo and Juliet*, Julia Kristeva writes:

> *If desire is fickle, thirsting for novelty, unstable by definition, what is it that leads love to dream of an eternal couple? Why faithfulness, the wish for a durable harmony, why in short a marriage of love – not as necessity in a given society but as desire, as libidinal necessity?*[84]

The problem is that love and the couple is always a problem, is always fraught with problems. Maybe it's because, as Freud suggests, in the narcissism of love, hatred is deeper and more ancient than love.[85] Certainly in Hardy's fiction, as in most fiction and art, bourgeois romantic love is presented as a struggle, where the lovers are in conflict with the social order (*Jude the Obscure*), with parents and the past (*Tess of the d'Urbervilles*), with neighbours (*The Return of the Native*), with education and background (*The Woodlanders*), and so on. As Cytherea says in *Desperate Remedies*, '"it is difficult to adjust our outer and inner life with perfect harmony to all!"' (13.3). 'As soon as an *other* appears different from myself, it becomes alien, repelled, repugnant, abject – hated' writes Julia Kristeva (1987, 22, also 1982). In Hardy's novels we see so clearly the simultaneous desire and revulsion – in the love affair of Sue and Jude, for instance, where the œdipal tension is in conflict with the erotic interplay of lovers. Love, for Kristeva, following the Freudian model, is a means of identification and abdication:

> *Amatory identification,* Einfühlung *(the assimilation of other people's feelings), appears to be madness when seen in the light of Freud's caustic lucidity: the ferment of collective hysteria in which crowds abdicate their own judgment, a hypnosis that causes us to lose perception of reality since we hand it over in the* Ego Ideal. *The object in hypnosis devours or absorbs the ego, the voice of consciousness becomes blurred, "in loving blindness one becomes a criminal without remorse"* – the object has taken the place of what was the ego ideal. (1987, 24-25)

Thomas Hardy's notion of love, as expressed in his fiction, is so firmly bound up with notions of art and artifice that one cannot discuss love in Hardy's work without mentioning how it is represented in art. For Hardy, the two modes of experience and ideology, love and art, are inseparable. In Hardy's concept of love, the myth of Narcissus is prominent: that is, the self-reflexivity of love, the *mise-en-âbyme* of love, the auto-eroticism of love, love as a crystallizing mirror in the Stendhalian manner. In Plato's *Symposium*, love is of/ for the other, the other half of one's being. One searches for the completeness to be found in the beloved. The beloved thus becomes that missing fragment which rounds out the desiring self. In Neoplatonism, there is a shift towards a different kind of narcissism. In Plotinus' *Enneads*, love is God, but God is also Narcissus. In Plotinus, the One is 'simultaneously the *loved one* and *love*; He is *love of himself*; for He is beautiful only by and in Himself.' (*Enneads*, VI, 8, 15) With Neoplatonism, a new kind of love is born, one founded on interiority and autoeroticism. Narcissus loves himself, he is both subject and object. His real object of desire is an image of himself, that is representation, art. Julia Kristeva writes:

> *He loves, he loves Himself – active and passive, subject and object... The* object of Narcissus is psychic space; it is representation itself, fantasy. *But he does not know it, and he dies. If he knew it he would be an intellectual, a creator of speculative fictions, an artist, writer, psychologist, psychoanalyst. He would be Plotinus or Freud.*[86]

The appearance of the lover, especially in late adolescence, can be very disruptive, as Tess Durbeyfield, Jude Fawley, Eustacia Vye and Hardy's other doomed lovers find out. Julia Kristeva offers remarks which apply to the fundamental sense of solitude at the heart of Hardy's fiction – that, after love has been enjoyed, and pain is to be endured, solitude is inevitable:

> *Erotic fantasy merges with philosophical meditation in order to reach the focus where the sublime and the abject, making up the pedestal of love, come together in the "flash." ...The contemporary narrative (from Joyce to Bataille) has a posttheological aim: to communicate the amorous flash. The one in which the "I" reaches the paranoid dimensions of the sublime divinity while remaining close to abject collapse, disgust with the self. Or, quite simply, to its moderate version know as solitude.*[87]

If art comes out of the 'crises of subjectivity',[88] as Kristeva suggests, and any number of artists' work could be cited to support her theory, then melancholy and solitude are inevitable. Melancholy is indeed the natural state of many poets and writers – especially love poets (think of Francesco Petrarch, Bernard de Ventadour, Giraut de Borneil, Emily Brontë, Emily Dickinson, William Shakespeare, Louise Labé, and others). The artist writes of love to bring back love. Metaphor becomes the mechanism by which love is reactivated, metaphor becomes 'the point at which ideal and affect come together in language'.[89] So important is writing and making art for some artists, that they are not really 'alive' unless they are making art. Many is the writer who does not feel a day has been spent well unless it has involved some writing. Writers often speak of feeling uneasy (or guilty) if they have not been writing.

Julia Kristeva's description of Fyodor Dostoievsky, in her study of melancholia, *Black Sun*, has some bearing on Hardy's fiction. Dostoievsky, Kristeva says, made suffering the keynote of his novels. But it was the 'non-eroticized suffering' of 'primary masochism', that is, melancholy. For Kristeva, Dostoievskian melancholia was 'the primordial psychic inscription of a rupture' (*Black Sun*, 186). Dostoievsky's form of suffering is 'neither inside nor outside, between two, at the threshold of the separation self/ other, even before this is possible' (ib.). In Dostoievsky's fictional world, which has many affinities with Hardy's fictive world, suffering, voluptuously, is essential; humanity is driven by pain, not pleasure.

Thus far, Kristeva's analysis of Dostoievsky relates directly to Thomas Hardy's art. But Kristeva goes further, suggesting that for Dostoievsky writing produces forgiveness. Dostoievsky, like Hardy, identified deeply with his characters (like all writers do). Dostoievsky thus 'travelled hell' with his characters (James Joyce's phrase), just as Hardy does with Tess or Jude or Henchard. The rebirth of the characters becomes the author's own. Writing is thus an act of signifying suffering which produces forgiveness, or as Kristeva has it, 'between suffering and acting out, æsthetic activity is forgiveness' (*Black Sun*, 200).

One can see how the relations between forgiveness, suffering and writing relate directly to Thomas Hardy's work. But asking forgiveness of whom? The mother, of course. It is the mother, or a mother-substitute, that the writer asks forgiveness of, according to Julia Kristeva. The mother is the one 'who has been killed by signs in the quest for individuality'. Forgiveness, then, is fundamentally equivalent to a reconciliation with the mother. This also fits in with the view of Hardy as a writer soaked in the mother-world, in the poetic evocation of (lost) maternal spaces.

All of the elements in the above discussion of love and sexual politics in

Thomas Hardy's fiction can be seen in his poems, in particular his love poems. The more well-known of the love poems include 'Thoughts of Phena', 'At Rushy Pond', 'Alike and Unlike', 'The Recalcitrants', 'A Second Attempt', 'Rain On a Grave' and 'He Prefers Her Earthly'. Each of the following extracts from Hardy's love poems offer extra dimensions to the erotic relationships in the novels:

> *The eternal tie which binds us twain in one*
> > *No eye will see*
> *Stretching across the miles that sever you and me.*
> ('In Death Divided', SP, 198)

> *When soul in soul reflected,*
> *We breathed an æthereal air.*
> ('Unknowing', CP, 58)

> *…that first look and touch,*
> *Love, doomed us two!*
> ('Last Love-Word', CP, 743)

In the poetry we get a deep sense of self, of the poet's self or persona, as the poetry is composed in the first person: thus: 'I have done all I could | For that lady I knew!' ('The Tree and the Lady', CP, 531), 'Woman much missed, how you call to me' ('The Voice', CP, 346). Hardy speaks of '[h]earts quick as ours in those days' ('A Two-Years' Idyll', CP, 628). 'Love lures life on' he writes in 'Lines' (CP, 458). And in 'After a Journey' he says:

> *I see what you are doing: you are leading me on*
> *To the spots we knew when we haunted here together.* (CP, 349)

The rustling of the gown or dress as one of the erotic marks of the woman (in *The Return of the Native*, for example), occurs in 'On a Heath':

> *I could hear a gown-skirt rustling*
> *Before I could see her shape…* (SP, 26)

In *Desperate Remedies* Thomas Hardy's narrator speaks of the acute sensitivity women have in their clothes: when Manston is standing next to Cytherea, she is painfully aware that her clothes are touching his: 'to a woman her dress is part of her body' (8. 4). Here is an early example of the 'hystericization of the body' that one finds in French feminism, where Hélène Cixous and Luce Irigaray speak of the whole of a woman' body being 'sexuate' or sexually sensitive.

The poem 'In a Wood' is subtitled 'See *The Woodlanders*':

> *Heart-half and spirit-lame,*
> *City-opprest,*
> *Unto this wood I came*
> *As to a nest;*
> *Dreaming that sylvan peace*
> *Offered the harrowed ease –*
> *Nature a soft release*
> *From man's unrest.* (CP, 64)

As the American feminist Camille Paglia put it:

> *A love poem cannot be simplistically read as a literal, journalistic record of an event or relationship; there is always some fictive reshaping of reality for dramatic or psychological ends. A love poem is secondary rather than primary experience; as an imaginative construction, it invites detached contemplation of the spectacle of sex.*[90]

This is why it is foolish of biographers of Hardy (or any critic) to assume that each poem describes a particular event. Hardy biographers are particularly guilty of claiming that this or that poem must refer to this or that moment in, say, the Hardy-Emma romance in Cornwall.

3

The Letter Killeth:
Jude the Obscure

Then another silence, till she was seized with another uncontrollable fit of grief. "There is something external to us which says, "You shan't!" First it said, "You shan't learn!" Then it said, "You shan't labour!" Now it says, "You shan't love!"

Thomas Hardy, *Jude the Obscure* (VI, ii)

Jude the Obscure (1895) is a sister (or brother) novel to *Tess of the d'Urbervilles*. The author attacks similar targets: the family, homelife, politics, religion, marriage, education and sexuality. *Jude the Obscure*, though, contains far more polemic and philosophizing than *Tess* or any of the earlier novels. The preaching and polemic threatens to undo the narrative, which is nevertheless 'realist', like other Thomas Hardy fictions. In *Jude the Obscure*, Hardy was stretching the novel to the limit, testing the boundaries of what is 'acceptable'. In *Jude the Obscure*, the things that say 'you shan't' are, variously, God, religion, society, education, circumstance, chance, nature, and marriage. All of these institutions and 'causes' reside inside the individual, which is what makes the problems they create so difficult to deal with for Sue and Jude. Patriarchy, culture and society are not in some 'out there' space, but inside people.

Hardy's thoughts on *Jude the Obscure*, as expressed in the *Life* and letters, include his desire for a novel about characters 'into whose souls the iron has entered'; a desire to make the story 'grimy' in order to heighten the contrast between the ideal life and the 'squalid real life'; the novel 'makes for morality', Hardy said (L, 273); and ended up 'a mass of imperfections', a remark many artists have made of their work (L, 273).

The title page of *Jude the Obscure* is usually printed thus:

THOMAS HARDY

JUDE THE OBSCURE

'The letter killeth'

Though not as problematic as the sub-title of *Tess of the d'Urbervilles* ('A pure woman faithfully presented by Thomas Hardy'), which seems to be a red rag for literary critics, the quote from St Paul, 'the letter killeth', is not as straightforward as it seems at first. However, whether one relates it to the potential destructiveness of religion, or Christianity, or Pauline theology in particular, or to the condemnation that society expresses in the name of religion, or to the idiocy of trying to live 'to the letter', the St Paul quote certainly sets up the religious tone of the novel. And not just any sort of religion, but a certain strand of Christianity, that of St Paul, which's nothing if not fervent and deeply felt. Some would call St Paul's theology mistaken, life-denying, sexist, violently dogmatic, sometimes psychotic, and even blasphemous in its identification between St Paul and Jesus ('Christ in me').

More powerful, though, is the polemical discourse in *Jude the Obscure* for being couched in fiction. Thomas Hardy is one of those rare artists – William Shakespeare, Dante Alighieri and Franceco Petrarch are others – who can combine poetry with politics in drama without making either discourse suffer. His fiction is poetic, dramatic and powerful while also being pertinent socio-politically. In some writers ideas and narratives mix uneasily (in for example the work of Aldous Huxley, Umberto Eco, Colin Wilson, William Golding and Thomas Pynchon). In Hardy's fiction the ideas and discourses are mostly fully enmeshed with the narratives. Part of the joy of reading him is to tease those discourses out. We regret that Shakespeare did not write a philosophical treatise, setting out clearly his life-view. How boring it would be, though, to have a single statement to explain all the plays. Much better is the mass of contradictions, games, side-trackings and glories of the works. It is so much more authentic. Those who demand a single philosophic statement that must never change do not live in the real world in which everything is changing. Nothing is certain, except the organic essentials (even those are evolving), and nothing remains the same. As Bertholt Brecht says, things will change.

Hardy pushes events to tragic extremes and climaxes. In *Jude the Obscure* he went as far as he could. Little Father Time's death is the furthest his rage pushed him. For many critics he went too far – right over the edge. Everything changes, though – twenty years later the Great War astonished everyone with its mass atrocities. In literature, seventy years after *Jude the Obscure*, we had William Burroughs. When Burroughs' characters are hung, they scream manically and ejaculate multicoloured venom everywhere. In the multi-secular, post-Sadeian, post-atomic world you can go as far as you like, because nothing is sacred. Two World Wars have seen to that.

Hardy went as far as the could in fiction with *Jude the Obscure*. His aim was not to shock but to draw attention to injustice and suffering. It is the same with William Burroughs. Both writers tried to go one stage further than their contemporary worlds, just as Pier Paolo Pasolini and Marco Ferreri did in their Sadeian satiric films.

The prohibition in *Jude*, just in a fairy tale, comes from the ancient maternal realm – that is, through Aunt Drusilla, who tells Jude Fawley repeatedly that the Fawleys are not the marrying type, or marriage does not suit them. As with legend and fairy tale, blood was spilt in the past connected with this family prohibition. '"The Fawleys were not made for wedlock; it never seemed to sit well upon us"' Aunt Drusilla tells Jude (I. xi). Later, Aunt Drusilla reiterates that anything more than being civil with Sue would be 'stark madness': '"If she's townish and wanton it med bring 'ee to ruin"' Drusilla tells Jude (II. vi).

After he has seen Sue in the flesh for the first time, and the erotic fascination has begun, Jude muses on the prohibitions that prevent him from marrying her: first, he's married; second, they're cousins; third, marriage in the Fawley family 'meant a tragic sadness', and marrying a cousin would double the tragedy: 'a tragic madness might be intensified to a tragic horror' (II. ii). These are apocalyptic terms to apply to something as everyday and apparently innocuous as marriage: 'tragic horror'. It is the terminology of wars and catastrophes, not marriage. It shows just how vehement are Thomas Hardy's views on marriage that he could see it as a 'tragic horror'.

Gradually, the sordid details of the previous generations' emotional follies emerge – the gibbet, the violence, the murder. As in *Tess of the d'Urbervilles*, what the protagonist thought was a sacred place, worthy of prayer (the Cross-in-Hand in *Tess*, the Brown House in *Jude*) turns out to be associated with violence and pain. Just underneath the surface of Hardy's Wessexworld is evidence of the loves and deaths of earlier generations. The place that for the youthful Jude was holy – the hill and the Brown House with its view of the far-off Christminster – is altered dramatically when Jude finds out from Aunt Drusilla that a gibbet once stood near the handpost. It is inevitable, too, that Jude should break the fairy tale prohibition; it is one of the functions of having it there early on in a story, that the protagonist should break it.

If in *Tess of the d'Urbervilles* it wasn't certain until the story was well under way what the violent pasts of the d'Urbervilles were exactly, in *Jude the Obscure* Hardy's narrator makes sure that the unholy past is clear. True, the narrator does let the Fawley history linger behind the action, without stating until well into the novel what the crimes were. The narrator teases the reader with vague information concerning the Fawleys. Such information always comes out gradually in such narratives. But in *Tess of the d'Urbervilles* it wasn't clear what the past follies were; in *Jude the Obscure* the narrator makes sure that it is understood that the Fawley's history concerned crimes of passion.

Marriage is the battleground here.[1] The discourse of marriage dominates *Jude the Obscure*. Every time Sue and Arabella meet without Jude Fawley (in Aldbrickham, and at the Kennetbridge fair) the subject is marriage; at the Great Agricultural Show, the overriding discourse is Arabella's musings on the Sue-Jude marriage; when Arabella meets her friend Anny at the Show Anny tells her she is soon going to be married (V. v). It seems there is no other subject worthy of discussion in the middle sections of *Jude the Obscure*. Every character relies on it for fulfilment. Sue and Phillotson have teaching to consider, but when Sue leaves Phillotson, his life decays rapidly. Jude only prospers, emotionally as well as materially, when he is with Sue. Secondary characters such as Widow Edlin and Gillingham further emphasize the centrality of the marital discourse.

Widow Edlin's opinion is important – it is not, like Gillingham's or Arabella's, on any particular 'side' in the central tangle of desire. Mrs Edlin's advice is common sense and plain-speaking. '"You are in love wi' t' other still! …You be t' other man's"' says Widow Edlin (VI. v). Sue knows it in herself but won't admit it to others. Mrs Edlin even commends Sue and Jude for trying to live without marrying, that is, trying not to make the same mistake twice. Widow Edlin intercedes practically at one point, when she tries to persuade Phillotson to delay the wedding.

(The name Phillotson suggests an affinity with *philo*, the Greek word for love, in this case perhaps referring to Phillotson's detached form of loving. Philo/ Phillotson might also refer, ironically, to *philo*sophy, which's pursued by both Jude Fawley and Phillotson. A more everyday affinity with the name Phillotson is Tillotson: it was W.F. Tillotson & Son who rejected *Tess of the d'Urbervilles*. Even successful authors harbour grudges over rejections.)

The 'experiment' fails of Sue and Jude. '"Perhaps the world is not illuminated enough for such experiments as ours!"' Sue muses (VI. iii). Sue Bridehead and Jude Fawley are described as being fifty years ahead of their time (V. iv). It's not *their* fault, Sue says, but society's – that it is backward, and can't keep up with them. Why can't society see, Sue says, that for such as us matrimony is 'the most preposterous of all joint-ventures' (V. iv). In the 'experiment' in erotic relationship of Sue and Jude, and in other relationships, Hardy was, according to a critic, 'telling his contemporaries that they had not yet imagined the human consequences of honestly living out the modernist premises' (D. De Laura, 1967).

Jude the Obscure is cyclical – the events go round and round but get nowhere. There is no finale, no climax, no endpoint. Each 'marriage' is supplanted by another one. Situations repeat, with no possibility of escape. The final marriage is no consummation of the narrative, as in traditional stories, for there is a simultaneous funeral.[2] The narrator's statement after the eleven year-old 'natural boy' Jude has been beaten by Farmer Troutham sets the tone for the novel:

> *Growing up brought responsibilities, he found. Events did not rhyme quite as he had thought. Nature's logic was too horrid for him to care for.* (I. ii)

The scenes where Sue and Jude try to get married are suitably grim – but it's standard to regard registry office weddings as lacking in 'poetry' (V. iv). The imagery of the sullen, reluctant soldier and his pregnant, battered bride is suitably sordid (V. iv); but even the middle class church wedding the lovers observe nearby doesn't console Sue. She comes out with a striking image of ancient blood sacrifice which D.H. Lawrence would have approved: '"[t]he flowers in the bride's hand are sadly like the garland which decked the heifers of sacrifice in old times"' (V. iv). Sue's harsh sacrifical analogy is echoed ironically later on, when she goes back to Phillotson. As the narrator drily calls it: 'the self-sacrifice of the woman on the altar of what she was pleased to call her principles' (VI. v).

At times all the fuss about getting married in Thomas Hardy's fiction – about 'putting up the banns', arranging licences, dreading the wedding day, rehearsing the occasion beforehand and capitulating at the last moment – can seem excessive. After all, in the XXIst century one could get married in Las Vegas with just an hour's notice. The marriage laws of the 19th century of course favoured men greatly. Phillotson would have been able to divorce Sue 'on the most facile of grounds' (R. Morgan, 1988, 135). Sue, though, according to the 1857 Statute, would have had to produce evidence that her husband had committed adultery, bigamy with adultery, adultery with desertion, sodomy, bestiality, or rape.

Neoplatonic ethereal love is fine until someone comes along and steals your man. When Arabella reappears at Aldbrickham, Sue goes into an apoplexy of sexual jealousy. '"Don't go now, Jude!... Don't, don't go, dear!... Don't! Please stay at home, Jude, and not go to her"' (V. ii). Again, the intensity of Sue's sexual envy shows just how important sex is to her. Sue would jump out of a window for the wrong man at the wrong time. '"It is torture to me to live with him as a husband!"' she tells Jude (IV. ii). Both Arabella and Gillingham tell Phillotson that a wife shakes down after a few years to marriage. Indeed, Arabella advocates that men 'chain on' women and treat them roughly (V. viii).

Thomas Hardy's basic point is that marriage can become a prison which traps people who should part. As he explains in his 1912 *Postscript* to the 1895 *Preface*, 'a marriage should be dissolvable as soon as it becomes a cruelty to either of the parties' (xxxvii). This laudable humane vision forms the centre of the book, but the view is often expressed vehemently. In the *Preface*, Hardy calls *Jude the Obscure* 'simply an endeavour to give shape to a series of seemings, or personal impressions' (xxxv-xxxvi). Often, the 'series of seemings' becomes an argument or tract.[3] *Jude the Obscure* is at times a soap box tantrum, which mars it, according to some critics, such as Virginia Woolf.[4] As with *Tess*, the main theme of *Jude* is intolerance and inhumanity, part of Hardy's 'long plea against man's inhumanity to man – to woman – and to the lower animals' as he explained in a 1904 conversation (F. Pinion, 1968, 178).

The first section of *Jude the Obscure*, 'At Marygreen', is immensely powerful: it is self-contained, a novel in itself, as it describes Jude's disenchantment with a host of subjects, from history, education and knowledge to sexual relations and domestic life. Thomas Hardy is on home territory here, ideologically and stylistically, describing one man's initiation into the complicated spheres of life, and his thorough disillusionment with them.

In the second part, though, 'At Christminster', things get more complicated. Again, sexual desire is at the heart of the complications in Jude's life, but a new force is at work – that is, Sue Bridehead. She is altogether more complex than Arabella. The narrative becomes densely intertwined at this point, and especially in Part Three, 'At Melchester', partly because Hardy has not quite decided on every aspect of Sue's character – how distant to make her, how sexual, how intellectual, how rebellious.

By the time of Part Three, the novel fragments into a series of journeys, which reflect the ideological, psychological and social fragmentation at the heart of the novel.[5] Many critics have commented upon the large number of journeys in *Jude the Obscure*. Railways play a large part in Jude's travels. The novel ought to be printed with a local rail timetable, as well as the usual map of Hardy's Wessex. One can spot the narrator consulting the train timetable from time to time as he relates the story. Following Jude's journeys is bewildering, as he trains back and forth between Christminster and his dying aunt at Marygreen, and nearby Alfredston, then going to see Sue in Melchester, then Shaston, having a night of sex in Aldbrickham, visiting a composer at Kennetbridge. Jude's all over the place. Sometimes he packs his bags quickly, leaves his job at one town, and goes to another. Decisions are made very quickly – he goes off with Arabella to Aldbrickham for sex at the third-rate inn after meeting her a few hours earlier after a gap of years.

The Oxford University Press paperback of *Jude the Obscure* prints a picture by Stanhope Forbes on its cover called *The Drinking Trough*, which shows a man standing next to a drinking horse. It is an image of rural calm. Far better to have a picture of a Victorian steam train on the front. The cover of Penguin's edition of *Tess of the d'Urbervilles* fares better: it shows a gloomy J.M.W. Turner watercolour of Stonehenge with a man in the foreground. This is still rustic and nostalgic, but the grim, embrowned Salisbury Plain is more in keeping with the tragic novel.

"I AM IN A CHAOS OF PRINCIPLES": MODERNISM IN *JUDE THE OBSCURE*

The restlessness, the eternal searching, the aching and questing for fulfilment in *Jude the Obscure* is typical of modern art. We see the same unease and yearning in artists such as Italo Svevo, James Joyce, Alice Walker and Toni Morrison. D.H. Lawrence summed it up in *Sons and Lovers*, where Paul Morel is a self-conscious development of the Jude Fawley personality: 'Paul was dissatisfied with himself and with everything.' (271) The restlessness of the modern artist produced many savage pilgrimages in the 20th century. For Lawrence, as for other expatriots, there was a visceral love-hate relationship with the homeland, Britain. It was a fascination and a revulsion, such as Aaron feels in *Aaron's Rod* (148). In Italy Aaron finds a 'bigness', a boldness, an exposed world: 'the walls of English life will have to fall' he thinks (ib., 239). A similar rebellion against England is found in *Kangaroo*, and in *The Insurrection of Miss Houghton*: England seen from a channel ship is described thus: 'England looked like a grey, dreary-grey coffin sinking in the sea behind' (*Kangaroo*, 286).

Thomas Hardy has not quite reached this modern/ postmodern state of weariness, although it permeates some of *Jude the Obscure*. On the whole, Hardy loves his Wessex and its people. His Wessexscape is a labour of love. *Tess of the d'Urbervilles* is his farewell to Wessex – he rounds off the kingdom there. *Jude the Obscure*, with its fragmented lives and train journeys, shows Wessex falling apart. In *Jude the Obscure*, too, Hardy's narrator's hatred of the mob shows through. He describes so incisively the way society cannot tolerate anything out of the ordinary. The animosity that the ever-so-slightly different love-affair provokes from their neighbours is brilliantly portrayed in the scene where Sue and Jude are painting in the church (it has to be in a church, site of the '"true religion! Ha-ha-ha!"' as Jude puts it, VI. vii). Various visitors watch the lovers and gloat. Sue cries out:

> *"I can't bear that they, and everybody, should think people wicked because they may have chosen to live their own way!"* (V. vi)

Things have not changed greatly in Thomas Hardy's world between his early and late novels, for by the time of *Jude the Obscure* Sue has to lie about the statues of Venus and Apollo, telling her pious landlady they are St Peter and Mary Magdalene (II. iii). Hardy is supremely economical again here. He turns the Goddess of Love, Venus, into the penitent whore of Christianity (the Magdalene is also a Black Goddess, associated with heresy, Gnosticism and occultism). Apollo becomes St Peter, one of the founding fathers of Christianity, and one of the people responsible for the hypocrisies of sin-sex-death buried at the core of the millenial religion. The pagan versus the Christian is often surpassed in *Jude* by a conflict between the religious (whether pagan or Christian) and the scientific – a battle between the old and the new, in essence. Hardy wrestles with these issues as his characters wrestle with their destinies in love and tragedy.

"A FANATIC PROSTITUTION": MARRIAGE

Marriage is the social battleground in *Jude the Obscure*. Thomas Hardy contrasts the secret compact between lovers, as found in occultism, courtly love poetry, the *Song of Songs* and other (often heretical) cults or movements with the public, legal, religious institution of wedlock. What should be a personal bond of 'hand-fasting' between consenting adults is turned, in Hardy's view, into a constricting, dogmatic socio-religious edifice.

The 'immortal puzzle', as Hardy puts it in the *Preface* o f *The Woodlanders*, is how to find a basis for the sexual relations between men and women (39). The 'immortal' sexual question is posed in *Jude the Obscure* by Sue Bridehead. If someone is suffering in a marriage, she tells her husband Phillotson, they should be able to be set free. For Sue, marriage is a 'horrible and sordid' undertaking. If the anti-marital tendencies in *Tess of the d'Urbervilles* had been proto-feminist, in *Jude the Obscure* they were directly and at times aggressively feminist. Sue's language is distinctly vehement: 'horrible and sordid'. No equivocation from her – though at other times she is less convinced by her thinking. For Sue, marriage is legitimised oppression and suppression, views with concord not only with mainly Anglo-American second wave feminism,[6] but also with postmodern feminism, as well as gay, queer and lesbian cultural theory. Sue articulates the oppressions of what gay theory calls 'hetero hell', where heterosexual couples are derisorily termed 'breeders', people whose function is to breed more people.

The intimate, secret feelings between two people become hardened into dogma and law: this is Thomas Hardy's polemic in *Jude the Obscure*. Passion becomes institutionalized. In the *Preface* to the novel he wrote of the 'fret and fever, derision and disaster' that can follow 'in the wake of the strongest passion known to humanity'; the aim of his novel, he said, was to 'tell, without a mincing of words, of a deadly war waged between flesh and spirit' (xxxv).

In Hardy's fiction, getting married can be a disaster of huge social, moral, religious and personal proportions. Listen to the language he uses to describe *Jude the Obscure*: 'disaster', 'strongest passion', 'deadly war', 'tragedy'. It is vivid, even apocalyptic language.

The tragedy of Sue and Jude is that there is no social or cultural space in which their special, two-in-one spiritual love can exist, let alone flourish. Their kind of loving is in fact tabooed by society: Hardy underlines the taboo by having them cousins, clearly evoking sister-brother incest, a feature of ancient Egyptian religion (in Isis and Osiris, Cleopatra and Ptolemy), and in esoteric movements such as Gnosticism, Neoplatonism and alchemy (the marriage of sun/ moon, silver/ gold, Venus/ Mars and King/ Queen).

Sue and Jude recall at times the mythical lovers of old (of course, Hardy would glow at the comparisons): Antony and Cleopatra, Héloïse and Abélard, Tristan and Isolde, Lancelot and Guinevere, Dante and Beatrice. Like so many lovers in fiction, Sue and Jude live their lives through the other person, as Cathy and Heathcliff do in *Wuthering Heights*. The cousin-relationship underlines the identity between the two lovers; when Sue dresses in Jude's clothes, she seems like a version of himself. In the manuscript of the novel, at the end of chapter three of Part Three, in a sentence that doesn't appear in subsequent editions, Jude sees in Sue 'as it were the rough material called himself done into another sex – idealized, softened, and purified' (440). The Melchester scene evokes crossdressing and Sue's playing with gender.

The narrator (and Phillotson) see Sue Bridehead and Jude Fawley as two halves of one whole – a Gnostic love-union of selves (called the *syzygy* [IV. iv]). In fact, their togetherness is very shaky. The dialectic of their love is continually shifting – from desire to disgust, and all the shades in between. There is no easy, simple dualism for Hardy. Sue and Jude drift apart and come back together in waves. They fuse then fragment, like particles in some sub-atomic experiment. It is a bout of Empodeclean Love and Strife for them, a state of Heraclitean flux, a Hegelian neurotic tension, shot through with the world-weary detachment of Schopenhauer. In Sue and Jude the big themes – the pagan and the Christian, the traditional and the modern, the spiritual and the sexual – are at war. Sue and Jude are the last in a long line of dissatisfied Hardyan yearners.

In *Jude the Obscure*, anything outside the norm of child-breeding heterosexual domesticity is slammed. Forget lesbian, homosexual, or other sexual relationships that challenge received notions of gender. There may be models and examples of Sue and Jude's spiritual form of two-in-one love in poetry, magic, religion, mythology and philosophy, but not in the towns and villages in which they live, in their immediate socio-cultural environment. This is Hardy attacking provincialism again: education introduces ideas from outside the community, which the community cannot integrate. Education unsettles norms, and creates (in Jude's academic aspirations) ambitions that cannot be fulfilled. At crisis points Jude reverts to his years of learning – he often, for example, quotes Latin, or the *Bible*, adding to the narrator's Biblical glosses on the narrative. Jude's hard-won knowledge is not, then, the parroting of a dead language, but an important element in his struggle towards creating an identity.⁷

Some of Hardy's bitterest pronouncements in *Jude the Obscure* concern Christianity. It is a text packed with religious statements and allusions. The epigraph of the novel, 'the letter killeth', comes from the most savage – and influential – of all Christian thinkers, St Paul: 'the letter killeth, but the spirit giveth life' (*Corinthians*, II. 3:6). In *Jude* 'the letter killeth' is treated with wrenching irony.

Jude the Obscure itself is a text in flux, reflecting the uncertainty and self-questioning of the era in which it was written – the time of John Stuart Mill, Charles Darwin, Friedrich Nietzsche, Arrthur Schopenhauer, Karl Marx and Sigmund Freud. Mill is a key influence on Hardy, perhaps the deepest influence on him among Victorian philosophers (M. Williams, 1976, 82). Mill's presence is particularly strong in *Jude the Obscure*. In *Jude*, all the old certainties – religion, family, education, friendship – are painfully shaken or lost. Christminster, once saluted by the young Jude as no less than the new Jerusalem, the possibility of Heaven on Earth, turns out to be a sordid place, where the colleges are compared to prisons and coffins.

A novel of failure, *Jude the Obscure* can be seen as offering a spectacle of torture, in which the chief 'victims' are children or child-like individuals (Jude and Sue are compared by Arabella to children [J. Kincaid, 140]). *Jude the Obscure* is a catalogue of failures. First Jude Fawley disappoints Farmer Troutham and is disappointed with the flaw in the scheme of things; then Vibert fails to bring him books; then he thinks of entering a Christminster college, and perhaps being a bishop; then he marries and that's a miserable time and failure; he lowers his sights again and attempt to enter the church as a licentiate, but that plan founders; he fails to capture Sue from Phillotson, and even gives her away to him; later, he burns his books; then his time with Sue proves frustrating – she remains unwilling to marry him; the two become increasingly ostracized from society; this is their time in the wilderness, during which Jude loses nearly all his former beliefs (V. vii); then there is the death of their children; Sue goes back to Phillotson; Jude is trapped into a marriage with Arabella; Jude decays further, eventually wasting away.

Jude the Obscure is a series of 'declining aspirations and the repeated checks upon them',[8] one failure after another, one compromise after another, with Jude being satisfied with less and less, until his death is seen by Arabella as merely an inconvenience as she tries to find a new mate at the Remembrance Day celebrations.

The failure of *Jude the Obscure* is built-in: Jude's 'obscurity' may be found in the novel's lack of unity, the fact that the novel cannot be resolved. Jude cannot realize himself, in George Wootton's Marxist analysis, because he is not acknowledged by his forebears and those he respects (such as the college dons). 'Where Jude turns he finds himself 'left out', literally unseen.' (1985, 104) There is nowhere for Jude – or Sue – to go. They do not fit in, there is no social or ideological unity in their lives. Hence, for three years of the story, described in chapter vii of 'Part Five', 'At Aldbrickham and Elsewhere', they lead an 'almost nomadic life' (V. vii).

'Events did not rhyme quite as he had thought' (I. ii): the sentence is understated but presages the sequence of losses and compromises that follows from Jude's early beating in the desolate sunken field near Marygreen. Thomas Hardy's project was to show the 'truth' – as a realist, rather than a pessimist. 'The besetting sin of modern art' he wrote in the *Life* 'is its insincerity' (224). *Jude the Obscure* is nothing if not sincere. Indeed, it is excruciatingly sincere, extending itself to the limit to render its tragic narrative. The utopian drive behind Hardy's realism makes him if not optimistic, then at least hopeful that things might improve. 'Opportunities should be equal all to all' he said, in liberal mood in the *Life* (213). *Jude the Obscure* records the apparent inevitability of inequality and its resultant misery. For this reason Hardy regarded *Jude* has his most 'moral book': it 'makes for morality more than any other book I have written' (L, 297). Hardy knew that his views were unpalatable for the establishment, especially when cast in the form of a novel (L, 302).

Like Jude, Thomas Hardy as a youth used to wake hours before he had to go to work (for John Hicks, the Dorchester architect) in order to read. In Summer Hardy rose at four to study until eight o'clock (*Life*, 31f). Like Jude, Hardy would sometimes speak aloud his thoughts as he walked – 'soliloquizing in Latin', for example. *Jude the Obscure* charts the quest that Hardy described in his *Life*: the search through 'various philosophic systems' for a life-philosophy that will work. This is Jude's task – and he fails. Jude passes from having (apparently) nothing to having something (Sue, love, a family, a job) to nothing again. It is the typical psychic trajectory of a tragedy, a rise and fall, except that Jude's and Sue's experiences at the height of their lives can be pretty meagre, and are usually modulated with blights and misery.

Jude himself, like Sue, is hopelessly romantic. He is so dreamy he does not bother for ages to make contact with the Christminster colleges.[9] Jude hopes against hope, like so many of Hardy's characters, that things turn out all right (Wildeve, Tess, Bathsheba, Viviette, Henchard). Jude has learnt early on that he can rely on no one, 'because nobody does come' (I. iv). Despite this realization, he goes to Christminster and becomes a stone mason, because he will be near the colleges which are made from stone ('only a wall – but what a wall!').

It takes a long time for Jude to wake up from his dreamy schemes. Jude's enduring faith in institutions such as Christminster, religion or education speaks of the œdipal, the patriarchal, the Kristevan symbolic. Jude remains for a long time under the Law of the Father. It is Sue who comments perceptively: '"[w]hy should you care so much for Christminster... Christminster cares nothing for you, poor dear!"' (V. viii). This is shown throughout *Jude the Obscure*: that however much one 'cares' for institutions, they never 'care' for you. Hardy saw Christminster as, yes, a 'tragic influence' in Jude's life, but 'innocently so, and merely as crass obstruction' (*Life*, 433). Christminster is definitely more than merely a 'crass obstruction', though.

Thomas Hardy's Wessex is not only a world of nature, emotion, personality and the spirit of place (the Hardy of the romantic 'heritage' novel, beloved of BBC serialization), it is also a world of great social change, in which the ideological forces at work are changing rapidly. The working class figures – Marty, Oak, Tess, Jude Fawley – try to cling on to the old ways of earning a living. Tess and Marty carry on working in the way they have always done. But they are overtaken by a new group of controllers, who have new methods. The way that Tess and Jude try to earn a living is far below what they are capable of doing. But Jude, pathetically, becomes a stone-mason, so he can be near the colleges in Oxford, so he can work with the very building-blocks of the colleges. Oedipal forces are at work here – Hardy's father and grandfather (the patriarchal ancestral ghosts) were both in the building trade. Jude calls the city beautiful even though it has gives him nothing (materially). Jude lives in a dreamworld. He buys books to learn, but then can't afford to have a fire in his damp room. He thinks the answer to his problems is simply to get money and book-knowledge. These are no answers, however. *Jude the Obscure* is the record of his journey towards the existential realization that nothing can provide an 'answer' to the human condition – not love, nor money, learning, God, religion, children, art, work nor even death. Jude the man begins his life in the world of late 19th century rural values, but ends up firmly embedded in 20th century anguish and self-disgust.

In *Jude the Obscure* Thomas Hardy takes on all of society. Hardy grapples, as Jude Fawley does, with the problems of paying your dues, of placating the ancestral and patriarchal ghosts, dealing with notions of genealogy and œdipal tensions. Hardy tackles Western philosophy, Christianity, hypocrisy, theology, paganism, materialism, ethics, morality and divinity. He tackles these subjects head-on. Many of the problems are unsolvable – especially that prime Hardyan theme of the reconciliation of the sexes, the attempt to find a meaningful and authentic love-relation. Hardy grapples with the whole process of enculturation – he tries to shatter it and examine it as honestly as possible. He falls into many epistemological and hermeneutic traps, but the struggle is glorious. *Jude the Obscure* is the novel Hardy should have been writing all along, from the beginning. It is his 'black book', a book of revelations, a manifesto and creative credo that lies at the heart of his whole work.

Gender and received gender roles play an important part in the economic and socio-political aspects of Hardy's Wessexscape. It is true that the women in his novels are too often stereotypes – the possessive mother, the betrayed maid, the neurotic lady, etc. The role of working women in a patriarchal society is a central concern of Hardy's fiction. He knew that women could be cruelly underpaid (Per, 186). In *Tess of the d'Urbervilles* he shows how a woman wanting to work on her own, outside of a domestic situation, will be the victim of all kinds of masculinist manipulation. Tess Durbeyfield is a prey to rape, hard labour, bad pay, patronizing male attitudes, patriarchal double-standards and an inadequate male-made justice system.

Though we think of Hardy's age as archaic, poverty-stricken and quite different from our own, some things have not changed. Women still earn on average 74% of what men earn. Poverty, disease, famine, slavery, prostitution and dictatorship are still at work in the early 21st century world. These problems are far worse now than they were in Hardy's era, because the number of people suffering is millions and millions more.

Jude Fawley comes from the ancient maternal realm. He lives with two wise crones, Aunt Drusilla and Widow Edlin. The more one considers Aunt Drusilla the more significant she becomes: she is the link back into the world of the maternal, ancestral past, a world that is valued so highly by Hardy and his narrators. Yet Jude's ambitions are for all things patriarchal and rarefied: the surrogate father, Phillotson, Christminster, Christian thinkers, the authors of the Classics, the *Bible*, the dons and students of all-male Christminster. There are hardly any significant female presences in Christminster, apart from two prostitutes in the tavern, and the woman who later 'prostitutes' herself, Sue.

Jude is on what anthropologists call a 'father quest', that archetypal strand of classic narrative where the death (or absence) of the parents sets a journey in motion. For a time Phillotson and Christminster function as a surrogate father or superego for Jude. All the aspects of Christminster are œdipally-related: the dons and students (again a father-son relationship), the books, the dead authors, the colleges, the education system. It's ironic that at the heart of this dry, academic, patriarchal city an ardent proto feminist, Sue, should exist. Not only that, but one who leads Jude back to the ancient maternal homeland. Though he leaves behind the mother-world of Marygreen, it catches up with him. The past, in the form of the family curses, eventually manifests itself. Like Henchard, Jude cannot escape his past: the book moves inexorably back towards the homeland, so that the final, climactic time Jude sees Sue is at Marygreen.

The novel opens with the quest for the father, with its œdipal struggles: to escape the family and the family 'curses'; to enter the Law of the Father and the 'symbolic order' of language and learning; this project is derailed by two women. First sex (Arabella) becomes more important for the initiate Jude Fawley than any amount of Greek and Latin classics, then spirituality and free thinking (Sue) overrides ambitions to become a licentiate or a student. It's inevitable that Jude's dream of a mythical continuity of culture and history, which's expressed in the night scenes of Jude wandering around Christminster and communing with the ghosts of the famous writers and theologians, should be smashed.[10] It is the wrong kind of dream, not a life-sustaining one.

Although Jude keeps alive his love for Christminster right to the end, when he returns to the holy city on Remembrance Day, it spectacularly fails to sustain him: he hears the concert but is shut out of the hall; he hears the Remembrance games from the river, and dies (VI. xi). No amount of learning saves him, and the city, the superego and Law of the Father, blithely carries on with its business, and he is ignored utterly. He remains an outsider to the finish. Sue says to him '"[m]y poor Jude – how you've missed everything!"' (VI. ii).

Jacques Lacan's philosophy of the phallus also bears on *Jude the Obscure*. Lacan's notion of the phallus as a signifier of absence is linked with death as well as the Law of the Father. *Jude the Obscure* is very much concerned with the 'Law of the Father', with the connections between death, the other, the symbolic, language and the Law of the Father. For Lacan, the sense of death comes from the bar to the real that the signifier sets up, or as he put it, 'the signifier as such, in barring the subject in the first instance, allows the meaning of death to come home to him. (The letter kills, but we learn this the letter itself).'[11] How accurately this describes Jude's ambiguous position, as one who loves language (culture) and wishes to pursue it, even though the cultivation of the letter brings with it the sense of death (and death itself for him). As Jude realizes so painfully in the course of the novel, the letter and the Law of the Father (the entry into the symbolic realm) is essential if one is going to be a human being, yet this entry is fraught with problems, not least being death-consciousness.

It's remarkable how similar the scene of Jude's return to Christminster is to scenes from the *Gospels*. Reentering Christminster has the subdued glory and moral ambiguity of Christ's entry into Jerusalem. Hardy's narrator prepared for this return to the promised land when he had Jude Fawley call Christminster Jerusalem in the opening chapters. Jude's speech to the crowd is verily a Sermon on the Mount. Except Jude's sermon is a typically Hardyan record of failure and disillusionment. In his under-stated fashion, Jude says 'I perceive there is something wrong somewhere in our social formulas' – that is putting it mildly. Earlier, Jude admits to the crowd that he is in a 'chaos of principles – groping in the dark' (VI. i). Jude's sermon to the Christminster crowd is an agony for Sue – Hardy's narrator gives a reason for her perturbation later on (she has seen Phillotson), but this is not the whole reason. For months – years – the lovers have tried to keep a low profile, and now Jude speaks to a host of people about his innermost fears and disillusionment. This sort of public admission is anathema to Sue. One imagines she would loathe American TV 'confession' shows, where the general public bares all to the viewing millions.

For Thomas Hardy's lovers, there is often one sighting of the beloved that remains in the lover's memory throughout their life. The beloved's 'characteristic scene', as Hillis Miller calls it (1970, 138), permeates the lover's perception of her/ him. Thus, Dick Dewy's first sight of Fancy Day stays with him throughout the novel. Sue appearing through a window, with the ecclesiastical attributes, in the centre of Christminster, remains with Jude throughout his life; so that, towards the end, when he is frustrated and perplexed by her sudden religious swerving, his sight of her as an ideal, pure, noble figure lies behind his statements of confusion.

It's apt too that Jude Fawley should return to Christminster, where he first beheld Sue, for she was the one figure that transformed Christminster from being a harsh, unwelcoming patriarchal city into something approaching the lost maternal realm, or at least a feminized world. Sue, as a Beatrice or *anima* figure, turns around Jude's experience of

Christminster as a difficult, inhospitable place, into something yielding, desirable, full of possibilities. Sue comes to be Christminster incarnate, to make fleshly the idealizations of the city that Jude had produced when viewing it from afar next to the Brown House. Jude's idealizing Sue as the erotic embodiment of Christminster of course is ironically shattered when, on returning during the Remembrance Day celebrations, they cannot find lodging because Sue is pregnant and they have children. Hardy's parody of the Holy Family entering Bethlehem and being turned away is bitter. Christminster is no New Jerusalem, from Jude's point of view, if it cannot accommodate enlightened individuals such as Sue and himself.

"LET US GO HOME WITHOUT KILLING OUR DREAM!": ON LOVE

Jude the Obscure is 'all contrasts', as Hardy intended.[11] A table of the opposites in the novel might include:

Marygreen	Christminster
paganism/ folklore	Christianity
no marriage/ love	marriage
individuals	institutions
flesh	spirit
sex/ sin	celibacy/ saintliness
Shelleyan love	legal, public love
materialism	spirituality
oral/ folk culture	written, printed word/ Word
Jude (youth)	Phillotson (age)
Arabella	Sue

A list concentrating on gender might oppose the following:

femininity	masculinity
matriarchy	patriarchy
Arabella's sensuality	Sue's spirituality

Hardy's text adheres, for the purposes of exposing the hypocrisies of his targets, what Hélène Cixous calls masculine binary logic, the hierarchization of society which favours the male.[12] For Jude, Sue at first appears as an *anima* soul-mate, an idealized beloved in the manner of Dante's Beatrice Portinari and Petrarch's Laura de Sade. Like Eustacia with Clym, Jude starts weaving 'curious and fantastic day-dreams' about his beloved. Interestingly, the narrator relates Jude's love for Sue immediately to Christminster; the emotion Jude feels for Sue is caused partly, the narrator says, by 'the poeticized locality he dwelt in' (II. ii). That is, the romantic appearance of Christminster directly affects Jude's love for Sue.

It's as if, living in such a lovely city as Christminster, Jude cannot help falling in love – and in an idealized, intellectual fashion, suited to the place. The spirit of the city breathes through him, erotically charging his intellectual pursuits, just as Sue later intellectualizes their erotic relation. However, the relationship is not simply Jude the courtly, chivalrous lover and knight admiring and exalting the chaste, spiritual woman from afar, as in the *amor lonh* of the mediaeval troubadours. There is much more erotic desire in Jude's love for Sue than he wishes to admit, and Sue turns out to be a far more complex character than Dante's Beatrice or Petrarch's Laura. She is more talkative, for a start, than ever Beatrice or Laura or most female beloveds have been in the history of poetry. Jude recognizes that his feelings for Sue are 'unmistakably of a sexual kind' (II. iv), a phrase that doesn't appear in Hardy's fiction before *Jude the Obscure*. Indeed, Jude muses like a psychoanalyst at times, using the terminology of psychology: 'it is not altogether an erotolepsy that is the matter with me' he tells himself (ib.).

Jude gazing lingeringly at Sue is a summary of all of the love affairs in Thomas Hardy's fiction, from *Under the Greenwood Tree* to *The Well-Beloved*. Jude gazes voyeuristically, in the classic Lacanian optical eroticization of the obscure object of desire, where the eye is a 'kind of phallus' (see J. Zipes, 1986, 258; L. Mykyta, 1983). In the Lacanian system of scopophilia, as post-Lacanian feminists have pointed out, male, phallic desire is affirmed, and sustained (see M. Humm, 1989, 84; L. Gamman, 1988; L. Mulvey, 1989). In Hardy's fiction, as in most love poetry and romantic fiction, it (love) is all done with the eyes and looks. Lacanians would say love (erotic desire) is all done with mirrors, narcisstically reflecting each other.

Just as Dante's *dolce stil novo* work or the troubadours' poetry was essentially a literary tradition,[13] so Sue and Jude's erotic relationship is highly literary and verbal. They talk about love more than doing it. They perform it, analyze it, deconstruct it, seldom indulging in anything as demonstratively physical as a kiss.[14] They intellectuallize their love, turning it into a cathedral. Their erotic relationship is an edifice built on a mass of religious, literary and cultural assumptions and allusions. Their love disrupts the continuum they once perceived between love and religion. Their act of loving fragments their own cultural environment, even as they yearn toward a Neoplatonic, abstract, etherealized form of loving, as recognized by their rival, Phillotson.

At the end of chapter two in Part Two, Sue is seen as a kindly star, an elevating power, a tender friend, a companion in Anglican worship for Jude (II. ii). These terms become ironic, doubly so, because Sue adheres rigorously to the tenets of early Christianity (chastity, abnegation, purity and self-abasement). The irony of Sue's initial anti-Christian thinking is pointed up in a series of rebellious gestures: buying the Classical figurines, preferring Corinthian to Gothic (*pace* Wardour Castle), preferring the railway station to the cathedral, and attacking the theological glosses on the most erotic section of the *Bible*, the *Song of Songs* (III. i). Sue's defence of the *Song of Songs*, wishing it could stand alone without the banal interpretations of theologians has a biting irony, because the *Song of Songs* is lush with eroticism,[15] yet Sue herself is very fastidious, sexually (according to Hardy in his letter to Edmund Gosse). '"*I* jumped out of the window!"' she tells Jude, twice (IV. v).

Laudable as Sue's attacks on Christianity are, it is one of the deepest tragedies of the book that she should turn about at the end, hanging her head and conforming. '"I don't regard marriage as a Sacrament"' Sue says (III. vi), yet she rejects her anti-patriarchal rebellion. Sue's psychological defences are built up throughout the novel, and smashed by her children's death. After that, Sue takes upon herself the blame and guilt for what happened. As with Tess, Sue has moments of nervous breakdown – her 'hysterical' behaviour at the children's grave, for example. Second wave feminist Kate Millett reckoned that Sue was not allowed to be both sensual and spiritual, the rose and the lily (1970, 133). Jude variously interprets Sue's apparent coldness as wilful or unconscious callousness, or as cold-heartedness, or as laudable chastity, or as frigidity.[16]

Thomas Hardy said he was 'more interested in this Sue story' than in any others he'd written.[17] Hardy exchanged some key letters about *Jude the Obscure* with his friend Edmund Gosse. Gosse in a review of *Jude* pinpointed Sue's sexual life as 'the central interest in the book'.[18] On the construction of *Jude the Obscure*, Hardy wrote to Gosse:

> ...there is nothing perverted or depraved in Sue's nature. The abnormalism consists in disproportion, not in inversion, her sexual instinct being healthy as far as it goes, but unusually weak and fastidious. Her sensibilities remain painfully alert notwithstanding, as they do in nature with such women. One point illustrating this I could not dwell upon: that, though she has children, her intimacies with Jude have never been more than occasional, even when they were living together. (I mention that they occupy separate rooms, except towards the end), and one of her reasons for fearing the marriage ceremony is that she fears it would be breaking faith with Jude to withhold herself at pleasure, or altogether, after it; though while uncontracted she feels at liberty to yield herself as seldom as she chooses. This has tended to keep his passion as lust at the end as at the beginning, and helps to break his heart. He has never really possessed her as freely as he desired.[19]

Thomas Hardy's explanation or apology of *Jude the Obscure* reveals some interesting points. Firstly, one sees that Hardy's narrator puts much of the 'blame' of the tragedy of the novel onto Sue. This is sometimes unconsciously done, for Hardy consciously exalts Sue. But he can't disguise the undercurrent of his opinion, namely that Sue's fastidiousness or 'weak' sexual appetite is partly to blame for the ensuing tragedy. It is not Jude's sexuality that is at fault. He is simply healthily lustful, which Hardy's narrator (and Sue) regards as 'normal'. Sue tells that Jude that his 'wickedness', his lust for her, was only 'the natural desire to possess the woman' (VI. iii). Sue thus condones the sexual predatory nature of men. Sue says of Jude that it is not sexual desire in itself that is 'wrong'.

What anti-censorship feminists say of pornography is pertinent here: Avedon Carol and Nettie Pollard maintain:

> *it is the fact that men feel entitled to make these demands which is disgusting – not what they desire sexually. This is not caused by depictions of sex acts in pornography, but by a sexist society that does not afford women full human or sexual status.*[20]

Sue is willing to continue to live as Platonic lovers, 'in mental communion'. Jude objects, saying that '"people could not live for ever like that"'. Jude seems to mean 'men' more than 'people' here, and Sue immediately replies: '"[w]omen could: men can't, because they – won't."' (VI. iii) Concerning sleeping with Phillotson, Sue says she has 'a personal feeling against it – a physical objection – a fastidiousness' (IV. ii). Sue's 'weak' sexual hunger, however, places her outside of the sexual norms, and causes the disruption in the Sue-Jude relationship. Sue simply won't fuck as much as Jude – or Phillotson – would like.

Marriage is sanctified rape, said the 1970s radical feminists. An extreme view, perhaps, but Sue is aware of it, eighty years earlier, in the 1890s, when she says marriage is like being licensed to be loved on the premises (V. i). For Sue, as for radical feminists such as Andrea Dworkin, Susan Griffin, Kate Millett and Mary Daly, marriage legitimizes the man's desire for sex. He must fuck her whenever he likes. The wife must always be available to him.

This feminist view of marriage and sex is backed up by an examination of the rape and marital laws from mediæval times onwards. Rape within marriage was not acknowledged: it was the woman's 'duty' to give herself up sexually to the man. It was not his desire that was seen as 'abnormal', but her partner's desire to withhold herself. Fucking is 'normal', and the desire to transcend fucking was regarded with suspicion in mediæval and Renaissance times.

One sees this suspicion in the plays of William Shakespeare, where characters are jeered at if they choose to go beyond sex. Celibacy becomes laughable from Shakespeare onwards in Western culture. You must put your genitals somewhere, is the socio-sexual assumption. You must live somewhere, you must eat something, you must have desires. One must fuck, is the assumption. It's the norm. A similar abhorrence of 'abnormal' behaviour occurs when people stress that they don't drink, or don't smoke. *What? You don't drink? What* are *your 'vices' or luxuries, then?* Everyone, it is assumed in patriarchal culture, must love sex, and have sex, or cigarettes, or drinking, or drugs, or some 'vice' or 'luxury'.

In his letter to Edmund Gosse, Thomas Hardy says that he was restrained by censorship from detailing the sexual aspects of the Sue-Jude relationship. And in "Candour in English Fiction" he complains about being censored, so that *Jude* was partly conceived as a way of destroying the taboo on 'those issues which are not to be mentioned in respectable magazines and select libraries' (Per, 130).

One wonders what Hardy would have written if he had not cared a jot about censorship or publication (critics cite Lawrence's *The Rainbow* as an example of what Hardy might have written).[21] Or if Hardy had written the novel post-1960, after the vindication of *Lady Chatterley's Lover*. Perhaps there would have been detailed sex scenes? One might have read about Jude Fawley going down on Sue Bridehead, and she pushing his head away from her clitoris, sighing, 'I just can't come today. Sorry.' We might have seen Jude badgering Sue for just one more blowjob.

Thomas Hardy shows in *Jude the Obscure* that you don't need genital details to portray the ravages of sexual relationships. You don't need to describe cocks and cunts, as D.H. Lawrence did, or dildoes and fist-fucking, as lesbian porn has done. The horror and revulsion, the desire and intensity of sex, is all there in Thomas Hardy's novels, without requiring the prose of soft (or hard) core pornography. It's an odd thing about literature, too, that Hardy was allowed by the socio-political climate of the late 19th century to describe in detail a young boy murdering two children then hanging himself, but could not describe the sexual relations between two adults. These curious double standards still apply to the media, where footage of death and destruction can be shown on the TV news, but scenes of 'sexual explicitness' are carefully policed.

Death, but not sex; physical violence, but not physical love.

Sue's sexual fastidiousness, her near-celibacy, is what keeps Jude lusting after her throughout the novel. This is what Thomas Hardy says in his letter to Gosse. In the same letter he writes:

> Sue is a type of woman which has always had an attraction for me, but the difficulty of drawing the type has kept me from attempting it till now. (ib, 350)

Jude the Obscure shows Hardy as definitely not the sweet pastoral novelist of *Under the Greenwood Tree* or *Far From the Madding Crowd*. *Jude the Obscure* is anything but a 'pastoral', rural, nostalgic novel. Throughout it, sexual angst is foregrounded. This is actually the case with much of Hardy's fiction. Hardy is labelled, wrongly, as a writer of rural England, who evoked some not-too-horrible rustic past. No. Hardy's fiction explores the connections between sexual agony and societal upheaval, between eroticism and class, between social ambition and parental pressure. *Jude the Obscure* investigates the horrors of going into marriage without really understanding what it entails. Sue finds out too late that Western bourgeois marriage involves the woman giving herself up sexually to the man. Sue has to learn the bitter truth about the idea of 'sacrifice' in Western marriage. In his essay "The Tree of Knowledge" (1894) Hardy said that

> a girl should certainly not be allowed to enter into matrimony without a full knowledge of her probable future in that holy estate. (Norton *Jude*, 352)

The most ironic – perhaps 'tragic' – aspect of *Jude the Obscure* is that both Sue and Jude make the same mistake *twice*, they both marry the wrong person *twice*. As if once wasn't enough, as if once hadn't taught them *anything*. To make a mistake of such grand proportions once, but *twice*? It is upon this deeply ironic act that the 'tragedy' of *Jude the Obscure* is founded. Both Sue and Jude are thus martyrs – not only martyrs to society, in society, because of society – but martyrs to themselves. Sue and Jude are martyrs to their own skewed notions of morality, to their strange, neurotic temperaments, to their misperceptions of social realities.

It seems as if Sue is the changeable personality – at least, from Jude's point of view she's fickle. Sometimes she's a New Woman, or a liberated thinker, or someone strangely superstitious about religion and marriage. However, Jude's sexual personality is equally in flux, as the whole novel is in flux. For Jude, and for Phillotson, masculine (sexual) identity is not a fixed, constant entity; sometimes Jude is a youth, overcome by erotic desire which swamps other thoughts (as when he first meets Arabella); at other times he is an abstemious would-be priest. Part of the socio-sexual confusions of *Jude the Obscure* surround not only Sue but also Jude and Phillotson: their (sexual) masculinity is under attack.

As is clear from the men's fate, masculinity is also seen as a social and cultural construct, with limiting and damaging qualities. Indeed, much is made of Phillotson allowing Sue to leave him for her lover, Jude. The populace of Shaston cannot understand Phillotson letting his wife go, though they are not surprised that she leads him a merry dance. The narrator emphasizes the heterodox nature of Phillotson's act, which he sees as an act of mercy. Phillotson, then, also contributes towards the questioning of sexual politics in *Jude the Obscure*, as well as the lovers.

If Thomas Hardy was the Secretary for Education of his day, he would have ensured that sex education meant more than learning about biology and contraception. Hardy, one imagines, would have classes on the power relations of marriage, the sexual demands made upon both partners, the way society views marriage, and the importance of being able to dissolve marriage at any point. The irony and often tragedy of Hardy's novels is that his characters are simply too young to really understand what they are getting themselves into when they marry so hastily. If Hardy was in charge of education, he would probably ensure that participants did not rush into marriage. Many of his tragedies stem from people following their desires impetuously, and rushing into marriage. If families mess you up, Hardy might say, then why dash into another relationship, such as marriage, so soon after teenage? Hardy sees marriage as bringing with it many demands that cannot be met. Hardy's basic advice would be: hold your breath and *wait*. Instead of, as Eustacia and Clym do, marrying after knowing someone for six months, *wait*.

From a Nietzschean, Western perspective, Sue and Jude fail to transcend the erotic dimension: they fail to sublimate their sexuality into spirituality. Despite all the talk in the novel, from both lovers, about the spiritual or idealistic aspect of their love, they never let go of the erotic component. Thomas Hardy says in the letters to Edmund Gosse, which provide the key gloss on *Jude the Obscure*, that Sue yields herself 'as seldom as she chooses', which contributes to Jude's frustration. 'This has tended to keep his passion as hot at the end as at the beginning, and helps to break his heart. He has never really possessed her as freely as he desired.' (R. Draper, 1975, 34) Although Jude retains his sexual desire for Sue until the end, as Hardy suggests, and Sue appears to be not particularly interested in it, sex is predominant in both their lives.

In calling Sue's sexuality weak and fastidious, Hardy can be seen as another male writer who underestimates female sexuality. For feminists such as Hélène Cixous, Luce Irigaray and Xavière Gauthier, everything has yet to be written about female eroticism – its 'infinite and mobile complexity' (Cixous), its 'all-over' or total-body erotic awareness (Irigaray), its violence, transgression, openness and fatality (Gauthier).[22] Though seen as weak, Sue's sexual identity is not described in the novel – it is one of the gaps or silences in it. Hardy could not, and did not, describe, for example, Sue's pregnancies, which may have been far richer experiences, for her, than getting married to Phillotson or having a Shelleyan, ethereal affair with Jude. Too often Sue is seen by the narrator as a desexualized wraith, a negative presence, sexually. The denials come often from herself, such as when she speaks of '"doing a penance, the ultimate thing"'. However, at this point, just before deciding finally to sleep with Phillotson, Sue tells him that she loves Jude '"O, grossly!"' The vehemence with which Sue suppresses her passion for Jude Fawley underlines further her high valuing of sexual love.

The trouble with Thomas Hardy's lovers is that they rely so much on love: they put all their hopes for fulfilment and happiness in love. They concentrate wholly on one person. There may be fifty thousand others with fifty miles that would also do, but no, it has to be The One. They're like kids who must have *that* particular chocolate bar, and no other. They expect that person to bring happiness, to complete their lives. This is the trap of late capitalist-consumerist Western society, which sees heterosexual, monogamous, labour-intensive, child-bearing marriage as the fulfilment of the individual. The characters that don't rely entirely on romantic, sexual love to make life meaningful end up happier in Hardy's fiction. The people who are deeply attached to nature, for example, such as Diggory Venn, are calmer and more stable. When Thomasin disappoints Venn, he has his trade and his nature-contact to fall back on. But Venn, too, is subject to the pressures of compulsory (hetero)sexuality. Hardy's lovers fail to learn how to compromise. They wake up from their dream too late. They don't think they're asking much – to love and to be loved. Yet their request proves as arrogant and impossible as any wish in Classical mythology or in fairy tales.

People are different: why doesn't society recognize this in laws, Sue asks. Why, Sue asks, should I not be who I am? Why '"should I suffer for what I was born to be, if it doesn't harm other people?"' (IV. iii). Phillotson, as the voice of stalwart, rational patriarchy, replies, no, you cannot be what you are, if it means not loving me. Phillotson uses an astonishing statement to persuade her otherwise: '"you are committing a sin in not liking me"' (IV. iii). These are the wild lies that a crumbling and increasingly desperate patriarchy tries in order to fix down the social and sexual fluidity of women. But, cries wounded manhood (Phillotson), '"you vowed to love me"'. Sue's reply is superb: '"[y]es – that's it! I am in the wrong. I always am!"' (IV. iii)

Sue argues that '[d]omestic laws should be made according to temperaments' (IV. iii). In the Parisian *L'Ermitage*, Thomas Hardy wrote a similar thing (in 1893):

> I consider a social system based on individual spontaneity to promise better for happiness than a curbed and uniform one under which all temperaments are bound to shape themselves to a single pattern of living. To this end I would have society divided into **groups of temperaments**, *with a different code of observances for each group*. (*Life*, 258)

Though Sue and Jude are meek, harmless personalities, they are punished. Sue cannot understand this, and neither can the narrator. '"If we are happy as we are, what does it matter to anybody?"' Sue asks (V.

iv). After the children's death, Sue reminds Jude that they intended, once upon a time, to 'make a virtue of joy'; but they were thwarted by civilization (VI. ii). The problem is that the reason Sue and Jude have been given such a shocking hit by the gods or by God is complex. For Hardy, in his utopian mode, 'individual spontaneity' is far better as a basis for a social system than a 'curbed and uniform' way of living (*Life*, 274). In the next sentence or so following this statement, Hardy changes his mind. But Sue cannot accept nature's law when it means 'mutual butchery'.[23] What a phrase, far more loaded than the 'Mutual Assured Destruction' of political nukespeak. The 'mutual butchery' Sue refers to is the death of her children, but suicide is not 'natural', it is a human problem. It is the artificial manipulation of natural events and acts that Sue (and Hardy) abhors. Sue says, towards the end of chapter II. ii, that the tragedy of love usually derives from 'a tragedy artificially manufactured for people who in a natural state would find relief in parting!''' (IV. ii)

In *Tess* the narrator, in bitter Shakespearean vein, speaks of 'shameless nature who respects not the social law' (XIV). The eleven year-old Jude found that 'Nature's logic was too horrid for him to care for' (I. ii). In Sue Bridehead's quasi-New Woman philosophy of love, people would be 'naturally' together or 'naturally' apart. Sue's problematizing of love largely derives from the far-reaching ambiguity of the word 'natural'. Later on, Sue realizes that the human conception of love exists amongst cultural beings, not 'natural' things like trees or animals. Her love with Jude is '"Nature's own"' but '"not Heaven's"' (VI. iii). For Sue, the death of her children tears open a terrible wound that can only be assuaged by the re-marrying Phillotson. The children's death is a sacrifice, she says, in order '"to teach me how to live!"' (VI. v).

When they are wandering for two and a half years, Sue and Jude are relatively happy – hence the narrator finds nothing much to write about them, and the years are summarized briefly. During this time, Sue is also relatively placid, as if traditional motherhood pacifies her, and the free-thinking 'modern woman' she once was recedes into the background. While Jude is undone by institutions such as class, marriage, education and women, Sue's deterioration is largely due to her sexuality, to the cruel laws of nature. Even as he attacks 19th century ideology, then, Hardy endorses its norms.

Jude the Obscure is a text in a 'chaos of principles', to use Jude's illuminating phrase (VI. i). There is no let up in the chaotic confusion of ideology, ontology, sexuality, psychology and religion for the characters – or for the readers. *Jude the Obscure* is an intense book, one to be read deeply but also quickly, as one might see a tragic play such as *King Lear* in one sitting.

The characters have different trajectories. Jude, 'the natural boy', has a fleshly disposition, like Alec d'Urberville or Michael Henchard. Jude loves sexual pleasure, even though he suppresses it. He tries to work towards civilization and refinement. The sheer strength of sex's hold over Jude is shown by his going with Arabella to Aldbrickham. After years of being in love with Sue, and not seeing Arabella for ages, he suddenly has sex with Arabella. Sue, meanwhile, begins very civilized and refined, but has to confront eroticism. Jude is incapable of acting properly. He can go to bed with Arabella, but cannot say to Sue 'no, don't marry Phillotson'. He'll have meaningless sex, but won't speak his mind to Sue, whom, presumably, he cherishes far more than Arabella.[24]

Jude Fawley is not the usual kind of 'tragic hero'. As James Kincaid notes, '[t]ragic heroes do not do such undignified things as jumping up and down on unyielding ice, trying to get themselves dead and failing.'[25] Jude does act pretty pathetically at times. Despite having deep romantic desires, he is often unable to act upon them. He prevaricates, he wavers, he yearns but remains in the same stultified position.

"KILL YOURSELF FOR A WOMAN": ARABELLA

Arabella is often portrayed by critics as a coarse, ugly, working class woman who has just one or two lowly desires. She is seen as essentially slothful; her ambitions run only to getting a man and keeping him so he can keep her in relative comfort. Even Thomas Hardy wrote '[w]ould not Arabella be the villain of the piece[?]' (L, 467). As critics often note, the first time Jude meets Arabella is when she interrupts his academic reveries by throwing a pig's penis at him. Arabella seems stained from her first appearance in the text by an earthy sexuality and brutish humour.[26] For (mainly masculinist) critics, Arabella is the sexual counterpoint of Sue; where Sue is refined, Arabella is coarse; where Sue is fastidious and puritanical, Arabella is open and liberal; Arabella has an 'ample' bosom while Sue has 'small, tight, apple-like convexities' (III. ix); Sue is first seen working on mediæval Christian art; Arabella is in a farm yard.

At many moments the narrator draws attention to Arabella's breasts, the emblems of her sexuality. It is, apparently, Arabella's breasts which unsettle Sue when she leaps out of bed. For Sue, Arabella's sexuality is literally too prominent, so Sue is unable to ignore it. Even when Arabella is a widow in weeds the narrator draws attention to her breasts.

Arabella, though, is at least honest with herself, about her motives and desires. She wants a man; she gets him, every time. She does not intellectualize her feelings, as the other three in the love-quartet continually and tiresomely do. Arabella does not delude herself: she appreciates sex and money as two of the key elements in a marriage, while Sue and Jude try to suppress such thoughts. Of course, Arabella is as much a 'victim' of compulsory (hetero)sexuality, like everyone else in *Jude the Obscure*. Arabella seems to know the costs and the joys of life, and dives in. Sue and Jude, meanwhile, twist and turn, moving forward, hesitating, backtracking, arguing, crumbling when events get too heated and difficult.

Arabella is the voice of practicality and reality; she tells Phillotson that women 'shake down' to marriage, if treated firmly. She says the same thing to her friend Anny early on in the novel, when she has been Mrs Fawley for a short while. Men always shake down, says Arabella: '"[m]arried is married"' (I. ix). Part of Arabella's function is to ground the high-flying, idealized views of Sue and Jude with some earthy commonsense, as Gillingham does with Phillotson. When Sue and Jude get all tearful from their lyrical intellectualizations of marriage and religion, Arabella's views bring the narrative back to earth, just as she did with Jude by throwing a pig's penis at him. Arabella's views concur with those of the narrator at times – especially when she is regarding Sue with her blunt but sympathetic eye. Arabella's view of Sue contrasts dramatically with Jude's; Arabella's practical view of life is summed up by her scathing view of the Sue-Jude romance: '"Kill yourself for a woman"' (VI. ix). Arabella, the voice of reason, cannot understand someone suiciding over a woman. Some of the more interesting scenes are those with Sue and Arabella alone together – the scene in the Aldbrickham inn, for example, when Sue goes to Arabella full of confidence, after having sex with Jude for the first time.

Sometimes Arabella's perceptiveness stretches belief: for instance, when she visits Jude at Aldbrickham and meets Sue at the door, Arabella perceives that Sue and Jude are not only not married, they are not living together in the sense understood by the general populace – that is, sleeping together (V. ii). It is a little far-fetched that Arabella should see all this from saying a few words with Sue. Arabella is articulating here the opinion of the narrator, who is in turn offering the received opinions of society. Sue and Jude's 'sin', then, is not only that they are not married, but they are not fucking each other. The working classes of Aldbrickham help to push Sue and Jude out of their town not only because Sue and Jude are unmarried, but also because, as articulated through Arabella's views, they are not having sex. Critics may dislike Arabella, then, because Arabella articulates what is hidden but understood in patriarchal society: the pressures not only to marry, but also to be seen to have an active sex life, or to want one.

The key scene of Arabella's ability to see Sue and Jude bluntly and earthily and mediate her views to the reader, is the Wessex Agricultural Show. Hardy could have chosen Phillotson here, but Arabella's practical vision presents a harsher contrast with Sue and Jude's idealized romance. '"Silly fools – like two children!"' Arabella mutters, not a little jealous (V. v). While Cartlett is not bothered at all by Sue and Jude's behaviour, and wouldn't even have noticed it if Arabella hadn't pointed it out, Arabella is troubled. All the characters who value sexuality (and marriage) highly – Sue, Jude, Arabella – are also troubled by it. Cartlett isn't bothered with Sue and Jude's ambiguous marital or sexual state, because those subjects don't bother him. Neither is Widow Edlin. But Arabella regards sexuality and its institutionalization in marriage as very important, so she is unsettled by sexual and marital ambiguity. Arabella speaks, via the narrator, for much of society, so not only is she as much a 'victim' as Sue, Jude and Phillotson, but most of society is the 'victim' of the overvaluing of sex and marriage. Hardy implicates the whole of society in his attack on the overvaluation of sex and marriage at this point in *Jude the Obscure* by having the sex and marriage discourse occurring in such a public, busy setting, the Wessex Agricultural Show.

In Arabella's character the biggest flaw is the development of her as a grieving widow who turns to religion, going about in black weeds for weeks after Cartlett's death. The 'conversion' to Christianity, and the sudden renunciation of it in favour of the resumption of sexual life echoes Alec's trajectory in *Tess of the d'Urbervilles*. Both 'conversions' and 'lapses' stretch credulity. It's the swift climb down (the 'fall') to sexuality rather than the difficult ascent up to spirituality that is easier to accept. Hardy's narrators are adept at portraying people falling from grace, as if his narrators secretly enjoy seeing people's moral aspirations collapse.

In Tom Hardy's Wes-sexual world, sexual instincts are immensely powerful, and can never be wholly ignored or suppressed. Angel's father, for example, does so – one sees vividly the suppression and sublimation of sex into spirit in the elder Clare. With characters such as Arabella and Alec d'Urberville, sexual desires are suppressed for a mere month or two: '"my wicked heart will ramble off inspite of myself!"', '"After all that's said about the comforts of this religion, I wish I had Jude back again!"', '"He's more mine than hers! ...Feelings are feelings!"' cries Arabella (V. viii). Indeed, 'feelings are feelings', and Hardy's fiction charts the eruption of these feelings, and the individual's – and society's and institutions' – inability to contain them.

The sexual politics of *Jude the Obscure*, like other Thomas Hardy novels, does not step outside of traditional heteropatriarchy. Hardy conceives of the opposites or alternatives in his sexual politics as being 'man' or 'woman', masculine or feminine. The third alternative – of the lesbian or (more correctly) the lesbian feminist cultural position – is not considered in depth by Hardy or any of the main Victorian authors. Alternative sexual identities, such as lesbian, gay and queer identities, hardly figure in a sexual politics dominated by two-term heterosexual logic. (But you can bet that had Thomas Hardy been writing in an era of openly gay and lesbian communities – the 1980s or 1990s, say – he would surely have included openly gay and lesbian characters in his texts, and tackled gay and lesbian issues and themes.)

Sue and Jude turn out to be thin-skinned, and more immature, socially, psychologically and religiously, than characters such as Widow Edlin and Arabella. Sue and Jude cannot stick to their decisions. They both marry the wrong person; the marriages are apparently dissolved; yet they cannot marry each other, even having many opportunities; the 'natural' marriage for Sue and Jude is never accomplished in the eyes of society and the law. The novel revolves around such cyclical and symmetrical structures: two wrong marriages, two re-marriages (both done in the early morning, out of sight of the public); Jude going to Christminster as an idealistic youth, and ending up there again in his last, defeated days; Arabella coming back and sleeping with Jude, followed by Arabella returning again, forcing Sue to sleep with Jude; two women turning to religion after bereavement; two women losing their high intellectual and religious ambition.

During the last section of the book, as all the trajectories begin to come full circle, both Sue and Jude quote or allude to the fiercest Christian theologian, St Paul, in particular *1 Corinthians*. St Paul fits in with the lovers' grievous self-immolation. '"I'm giving *my* body to be burned"' laments Jude (VI. vi). Sue's 'burning' is Hardy's most bleak living death. Sue and Jude meet near the Martyrs' Cross in Christminster and towards the end Jude staggers past it with Arabella. Jude aligns himself with the Oxford Martyrs, and thus exalts himself in the eyes of religion, just as Sue does. Sue and Jude end up as martyrs – but martyrs partially to their own highly idealistic form of love, as well as to institutions such as marriage, the family, religion and society.

In the last part of *Jude the Obscure*, St Paul takes over from Percy Bysshe Shelley, and the ghosts of Christminster/ Oxford return to haunt and taunt Jude. '"They seem laughing at me!"' moans Jude (VI. ix) during the bitter re-run of Jude's entry into the New Jerusalem. He reels off the names of the illustrious 'sons' of the Christminster – Browne, Bacon, Raleigh, Arnold, Johnson – and Arabella stops her ears. Even now, beaten and exhausted, Jude still regards the Christminster *illuminati* highly, so they can unsettle him and he thinks they're laughing at him. '"I'm an outsider to the end of my days!"' he sighs (VI. i). Jude's deep respect against all the odds is just like Sue's respect for religion and the institution of marriage which forces her to do the 'ultimate thing' with Phillotson.

In the final section of *Jude the Obscure*, 'At Christminster Again', Hardy piles on one pathetic event after another. Jude Fawley standing outside the theatre in the rain hoping to catch some of the Latin speeches is but the beginning of the degradations (VI. i). There is the trudging around the lodgings; the hopeless conversation between Sue and Little Father Time, which echoes Tess's talk with her younger brother about the blighted planet; then the death of the children; then Sue's intense recriminations; the funeral; Sue trying to see her children in their coffins; Sue giving birth to a dead baby; Sue mortifying herself further ('"[w]e should mortify the flesh – the terrible flesh – the curse of Adam!"' VI. iii); the return of Arabella; Sue and Jude parting; Sue's re-marriage to Phillotson; Jude's decline; the drunken days at Arabella's father's house and the re-marriage; to see Sue for the last time; Sue going to Phillotson's bed; Jude's death.

That chapter – VI, ii – of *Jude the Obscure* is Thomas Hardy's most severe, grotesque, tragic or tragi-comic, depending on how you look at it. 'All tragedy is grotesque – if you allow yourself to see it as such' wrote Hardy in the *Life* (315). Though Little Father's Time death is extraordinary – and especially when he kills his brothers and sisters too, there have been cases not unlike Hardy's near-sick event.[31] Hardy's narrator, though, notes that Sue makes at least two major mistakes in the events leading up to the children's death – again, 'the woman pays', as in *Tess of the d'Urbervilles.* '"The woman mostly gets the worst of it in the long run!"' says Jude (VI. iii).

The first 'mistake' is to talk gloomily with little Jude about life being all 'trouble, adversity and suffering' (VI. ii). Given Little Father Time's sombre disposition, it would be easy enough to slip into a morbid tone in conversation with him, for Sue is melodramatically negative at times. Sue's second mistake is to leave the children unattended. Arabella does the same with Jude – leaving him alone instead of waiting until her father arrives. Sue leaving her children alone is more dangerous, though, for Jude is dying anyway, and he's an adult. One would have thought that a boy could have been found to run a message across to Jude – there always seems to be messengers available in Hardy's fiction, just as there seem to be ten different postal deliveries per day. But no, Sue leaves the children – at 'a little past six'; when she returns with Jude, the children are dead. Thus the tragedy partly arises from Sue abandoning one of the prime function of women in a patriarchal state: being a good mother, looking after her children.

Phillotson's progressive ideas on single parenthood, which so startle the voice of reason (Gillingham) do not last. When Sue returns to him, Phillotson says that their 'half-marriage should be completed' (VI. ix). That is, Sue should have sex with him. Phillotson's liberal views are dropped in favour of upholding male-female power relations through sex. The images of Sue screwing herself up to a point of utter suppression in order to have sex with Phillotson are the most gut-wrenching in *Jude the Obscure.* '"It is my duty. I will drink my cup to the dregs!"' she tells Mrs Edlin (VI. ix). Earlier, Hardy showed the vehemence of Sue's capitulation by having her tear up her nightdress and burning it. Mourning their failed love, Jude alludes to the veil of their temple being rent – the ripping up of Sue's nightdress, emblem of their former erotic life, is clearly related to the rent temple veil image. The two edifices – sex and religion – crumble simultaneously in *Jude the Obscure.* A small visual detail indicates Sue's suffering at this point, when she has finally decided to sleep with

Phillotson. She has already blenched on seeing the marriage licence (always a document of doom in Hardy's fiction, and especially so in *Jude the Obscure* – the licence reminds her of the sordid, materialistic nature of marriage); she has shrunk from Phillotson's kiss; now, as Phillotson prepares to lift her up, to carry her into his bedroom, just as bridegrooms are supposed to do across the threshold, Sue shrinks from him a final time. The narrator continues: 'he led her through the doorway, and lifting her bodily he kissed her. A quick look of aversion passed over her face, but clenching her teeth she uttered no cry.' (VI. ix) The teeth clenching acutely describes Sue's suppression of her abhorrence of the 'ultimate thing'. 'In presenting herself at [Phillotson's] bedroom door she is demonstrating the full hideous iniquity of conventional marriage which is Hardy's target in the novel' (K. Millett, 133). At this point, just as the action is with Sue being carried into Phillotson's bed chamber, Hardy's narrator moves swiftly aside, as he did just when Tess was about to be raped, and turns to Widow Edlin wondering if she should check on Sue one more time.

Churches feature prominently in *Jude the Obscure,* and nearly always ironically: there is the ugly new church at Marygreen which replaced the beloved old village structure; the smaller churches in the suburbs of Christminster (such as St Silas); and the rarefied interiors of two cathedrals: Melchester (Salisbury) and Cardinal (Christchurch) College's cathedral. Significantly, Cardinal College's cathedral has a Norman interior which Sue lays into as being barbaric. Two of the key last meetings between Sue and Jude take place in churches, as Hardy increasingly emphasizes the religious or spiritual dimension of their failed 'experiment'.

In *Tess of the d'Urbervilles* the narrator describes the acts of the man who paints Christian slogans on Sundays as 'the last grotesque phase of a creed which had served mankind well in its time' (XII). In *Jude the Obscure,* Thomas Hardy is even more severe about Christianity, laying into it at every opportunity. In his *Life* he said hadn't found God after looking for Him for 50 years (234), but Sue clutches onto religion, despite her better judgement. 'We must conform! …we must submit. There is no choice. We must. It is no use fighting against God!' (VI. iii) This comes from a character who is sometimes virulently anti-Christian. Jude reminds her of this, and Sue admits she is feeling 'as superstitious as a savage!' (ib.)

Where is God, anyway? By the time of *Jude the Obscure* (1895), after Charles Darwin and Friedrich Nietzsche had declared Him dead, and Sigmund Freud was beginning to publish his findings, God was inside people, if anywhere. The Divine was made by people, for people. Sue, if anyone in the novel, should know that. She does know it, but still she reverts, incredibly, to Christian teaching.

In the last part, the opposites of the novel become even more aggravated: between being single and being a parent; between having no responsibilities and having many; between Shelley and St Paul; between ancient and modern; between Christminster and Marygreen; between chastity/celibacy and sexual activity, and so on. For Jude, their 'tragedy' is human-made – God doesn't enter into it ('"[i]t is only against man and circumstance"' he says, VI. iii).

Chapter VI. iii contains Hardy's bitterest attacks on Christianity, when Sue starts visiting St Silas church. Sue becomes more like Christ than Jude (although Jude is likened to Jesus throughout the novel (pp. 35, 93, 109, 127, 134, 253, 348, 373, and Sue compares him to Joseph the dreamer, St Stephen and Don Quixote, IV. i)).

Sue is more Christ-like than any of Hardy's previous characters (Angel, Clym, Giles, Oak). She wishes to atone for all sins, and especially her 'fall'. Sue cuts through two thousand years of Christianity, to return to the extreme asceticism of the early Christians, especially the Gnostics and heretics who mortified their flesh in extraordinary ways (living in caves, up poles, in pits, flagellating themselves, wearing hair shirts, and so on). '"Self-renunciation – that's everything! I cannot humiliate myself too much"' Sue cries (VI. iii). She says they have not 'insulted' their first marriages by remarrying. At this point, Jude begins to realize that Sue is changing her moral views. A similar recourse to an earlier marriage occurs in *Tess of the d'Urbervilles*, when Tess, to her partner's (Angel's) surprise, begins to regard her first relationship (with Alec) as more 'natural' (or, oddly, more socially sanctified) than her present one to Angel.

Jude's desperation increases through chapter three of Part Six of *Jude the Obscure*, as he realizes that Sue's views are diverging from his more and more. The notion of 'sin' is one of the most life-killing ideas in the post-Classical world. Indeed, the Christian emphasis on 'sin', especially in St Paul, was abhorrent to the ancient Greek and Jewish world. In *Jude the Obscure*, Hardy shows how ridiculous Christian 'sin' is, when it won't allow Sue and Jude's 'natural' (Neoplatonic) two-in-one marriage. Sue regards their marriage as 'Heaven's, not Nature's' (ib.). Jude cannot understand Sue's 'conversion' to Pauline Christianity: for him, Sue, such a shining 'woman-poet, a woman-seer' is degrading herself (ib.).

Jude clings onto the idea of love as a magical, Shelleyan, Neoplatonic, romantic experience more sacred than the spiritual marriage or *hieros gamos* offered by Christianity. For Jude, their relationship is 'one of the highest and purest loves that ever existed between man and woman' (ib.). Earlier in the novel, Sue mentions the Platonic form of loving symbolized by Venus Urania (III. vi). But, as usual in Hardy's world, later, Christian laws wind up dominant, and the nostalgic affection for earlier, Classical forms of loving are not sustainable.

The emphasis on the first, religious marriage, which Sue regards as truer than her second 'marriage' with Jude, is echoed in *Far From the Madding Crowd*. At the crucial coffin scene, when Bathsheba confronts Troy with his betrayal, he says that he is more 'morally' Fanny's than hers. Bathsheba is horrified, and emits 'a long low cry of measureless despair and indignation, such a wail of anguish as had never before been heard within those old-inhabited walls' (XLIII). Oddly pious all of a sudden, Troy addresses the dead Fanny Robin: '"in the sight of Heaven you are my very, very wife!"' Sue uses exactly the same terms to justify the significance of her marriage with Phillotson. The recourse of Sue to Christianity is understandable, but in Troy it's bizarre. Troy asks Bathsheba when they first meet: '"are you a woman?"' the answer the text gives is that Fanny is 'more' of a woman than Bathsheba. Fanny has at least given Troy a child, one of the marks of 'womanhood' for patriarchy.

In an era in which pornography blossomed into a mass industry, and prostitution was rife (S. Marcus, 1969), Thomas Hardy's views that marriage, that holy sacrament and institution, could be a 'fanatic prostitution' (J, VI. iv) were startling. (Kate Millett speaks of Sue's 'final psychotic self-mutilation', 133). The irony is that these views come not from the one-time free thinker, Sue, but from Jude. He is thinking of Phillotson possessing her sexually – it is his sexual jealousy that causes him to say to Sue that going back to Phillotson will be a 'fanatic prostitution'. Yet these radical views are also those of Hardy's narrator. It is the logical end result of second wave radical feminism that marriage can be seen as sanctified prostitution; it is unusual to find such a view in the 1890s, and this is partly why *Jude the Obscure* is such a 'modern' novel. (Kate Millett's analysis of *Jude the Obscure* is typical of such second wave feminism: '[w]hat lies at the root of her capitulation is patriarchy's ancient masochistic system: sex is female and evil' 132).

Jude starts asserting that Sue is his wife 'in all but law': he states this a number of times, and each time, Sue rebuts him. For Jude, Sue is his wife – he has regarded her as such for years. He sees her as his 'natural' (= sexual) or 'common law' wife, yet he also knows, secretly, that they are not viewed as such by society. Indeed, it was Jude who kept encouraging Sue to marry him, and she who kept swerving at the last minute. It is as if Sue was thinking ahead to the time when they would have to part.

Sue says that even if they married, she would still be Phillotson's wife. No wonder Jude is pained by her remarks: Sue says: '"I feel more and more convinced as time goes on that – I belong to him, or to nobody!"' (VI. iii) It is this last point that drives the knife in, for it sweeps away all the time Sue has spent with Jude. It is as if he and their love have never been. Jude says '"[h]ow you argued that marriage was only a clumsy contract – which it is – how you showed all the objections to it – all the absurdities."'

Both of the lovers blame themselves for the failure; Jude takes it personally, as if Sue is attacking the quality of his loving, his sexual identity: '"[y]ou have never loved me as I love you – never – never!"' Jude harps on this note of selfishness, when he implores Sue not to abandon him to his two vices, women and drink. '"Don't abandon me to them, Sue to save your own soul only!"' he cries (VI. iii).

In this chapter the lovers use every trick of suasion to achieve their desires. The chapter is like a miniature theatrical play, a one act drama on the death of love. Seen as a middlebrow melodrama, Jude's next act – to pick up a pillow from the love-bed and throw it on the floor – is the behaviour of a petulant, childish lovelorn teenager. Indeed, both lovers act like children, immaturely evaluating their ever-shifting emotional positions. The isolated acts can seem silly and adolescent – but when they're put into the whole dour, weighty narrative of *Jude the Obscure*, they become pregnant with emotional resonance. This is – again and again this is to be seen – Hardy's triumph: to take seemingly ordinary events and lives and make them resonant, even 'tragic'. These acts and dialogues seem trivial – whether to kiss or not, for example – yet Hardy's texts invest them with grandeur. And Hardy's narrators have long known how to aggrandize dialogue with a Biblical reference or two (or three hundred).

For example, at the moment when Jude flings the pillow to the floor, he evokes that gargantuan moment in the Christian Passion when the veil of the temple is rent in twain, the moment of Christ's death. Thus the tear or wound that opens in the veil of the lovers' Platonic or 'spiritual' marriage has, from Jude's viewpoint, a powerfully sexual component, which he can't – and won't – ignore. Jude's pillow-throwing is an act of desecrating the temple of the love-bed, where they have shared their Platonic two-in-oneness. For Jude, the rent temple veil is a wound in their sexual life which is never afterwards healed. He sees their problem as pivoting around sex. Or rather, he sees that Sue's leaving him will mean sexual deprivation for him.

After the calamitous dialogues in chapter VI. iii, Jude tries again to assert that Sue is his wife. '"But you are *my* wife!"' And again Sue tells Jude that even if they *had* got married, she would feel the same. At this point, for Jude, Sue's admission that she is going back to Phillotson is devastating; but just as incredible for him is Sue telling him she is going to re-marry Phillotson. She will willingly marry Phillotson *twice*, but not him once. He can't believe it.

Sue, meanwhile, is desperately trying to mend her life, and casts herself in the role of '"a poor wicked woman who is trying to men"' (VI. iv). Sue will not 'lie or die' in patriarchy – she always wishes to tell the truth. This laudable trait contributed, as she admits, towards the death of her children: '"[i]t was that I wanted to be truthful. I couldn't bear deceiving him [Little Father Time] as to the facts of life' (VI. ii). Sue's truthfulness is partly what creates such pain in herself as in Jude, as when she tells him she is marrying Phillotson even though she doesn't love him (VI. iv). Sue's adherence to rigour and being truthful is, ironically, what disrupts the Platonic two-in-oneness, and the lives of the main characters.

Their last meeting, at their family's homeland, the Marygreen area, takes up two pages of dialogue which is, as one would expect, full of breathless phrases, promises, and much use of 'O' and exclamation marks. Again, Jude Fawley makes assertions of possession ('"*His* wife. You are mine"'), and again Sue quivers on the point of renouncing her renunciation and going back to Jude. Sue swerves between restraint and passion. She says she has '"nearly brought my body into complete subjection"', an extraordinary admission. The Pauline Christian austerity has gripped hold of her severely. Yet her self-denial, like his, has not brought about the spiritual transformation she wishes for. In the taunting, romantic, would-be tragic conversation that ensues in Marygreen church, each lover veers from extreme to extreme, delight to disgust, denial to desire. Sue's eroticism is just as powerful as Jude's here, as at other times. Rather than being the 'fastidious' person Hardy depicts her as in his letter to Edmund Gosse, Sue not only desires to be loved, but requires the erotic confirmation of love in passionate kisses. '"Kiss me, O kiss me lots of times"'. It is then that she tells him she has not been sleeping with Phillotson, but the marriage has been a 'nominal' or 'apparent' one. This news naturally cheers Jude up no end, for he, like, Sue, like all of society, values sexual acts very highly.

Jude's mistake is to kiss her in memory of their dead children. This is too much for Sue: kissing a dying lover when one is married to another is one thing, something doom-laden but also sensuous and romantic. Sue can kiss Jude like that and somehow justify it, despite her spiritual renunciation. When he mentions the children, though, it goes too far. The children's death was the act that rent their temple vein in twain, the never-healed wound between them.

The children's death adds a weighty new responsibility to the love tragedies between two people. Instead of two people swooning and kissing and pledging themselves to each other beyond death and to all eternity, children mean new souls and bodies to consider, with consequences far beyond the relationship of two lovers. It is this dimension of social responsibility that Hardy seldom explored: the addition of parental responsibility to that of heterosexual lovers. It is significant that, even in *Jude the Obscure*, a novel with a sizeable component of parent-child relationships, the narrative should still concentrate on romantic love. So that the children are only mentioned towards the end of Sue and Jude's last ever meeting. Despite having three children (one was in Sue's womb), plus Little Father Time, they are hardly mentioned in the conversations that take place some time after their death. When Jude mentions them, he re-introduces the ever-painful subject of their death, the event which reminds Sue that they were, in her words, 'sin-begotten', a sacrifice that encouraged her self-purification. Jude then tries for the last time to persuade Sue to come away with him, the theme of Hardy's bitter poem 'The Recalcitrants':

"We've married out of our senses. I was made drunk to do it. You were the same. I was gin-drunk; you were creed-drunk. Either form of intoxication takes away the nobler vision. Let us then shake off our mistakes, and run away together!" (VI. viii)

Jude and Sue see themselves as ahead of their time, but the problem for the recalcitrants is that they 'are constructed by the very terms they seek to transcend', as Elizabeth Langland put it.[32] They cannot live outside the law, either natural or social. The law will always ultimately coerce them into particular actions or ideologies. Constructing one's own law or world is not possible in *Jude the Obscure*. Social construction leads to bodily destruction. 'The lingering sadness of this novel lies in its apprehension of the ways destructive cultural self-constructions ultimately reach out to claim them' remarked Elizabeth Langland (ib., 46). At first, the 'natural' law in *Jude the Obscure* seems precede the social law, but by the end of the book, the two laws, natural and social, 'are threatening to collapse into one'. Consequently, '[t]here is no authentic possibility of a life outside of the law in *Jude*' (W. Goetz, 213).

Sue Bridehead's portrait is drawn by the narrator via Jude Fawley's new feelings about her: she is mobile, slight, elegant, short (II. ii). Aunt Drusilla fills in more of her history in chapter II. vi: the way Sue pulled her petticoats over her knees and walked into the village pond; her impertinence, which made Aunt Drusilla smack her many times; Sue is called a 'pert little thing', with 'tight-strained nerves'. Like Jude, Sue has the ability to imagine things vividly, so that they could almost be seen in front of them. Sue was a performer, revelling in reciting Edgar Allen Poe's 'The Raven'. She was something of a tomboy, playing with the village boys, on her own amongst twenty boys.

Sue is not 'modern', she says, nor is she 'mediæval': she tells Jude she is 'more ancient than mediævalism"' (III. i). There is an element in Sue's character that goes back to ancient times, to a pre-Christian, pre-Fall era, somewhere paradisal, before the complications of sex and sin had set in. It is expressed in her penchant for the very ancient, for the Greek statues, for the Corinthian over the Gothic, for the simple pleasures of the roses. For Jude, such a heightened and subtle enshrinement of the childlike often goes beyond his understanding and can seem frustratingly like being childish. A few pages later, during the Wardour Castle jaunt, Sue says she is not 'civilized' in the traditional sense, but craves 'to get back to the life of my infancy, and its freedom"' (III. ii).

Sue's fate demonstrates vividly (as does Tess's, and Thomas Hardy's other women) Simone de Beauvoir's famous dictum in *The Second Sex*: '[o]ne is not born, but rather becomes, a woman'. Hardy's attitude towards Sue, or his narrator's attitude towards her, has long confused critics. Though Hardy's narrator is largely on Sue's side, when it comes to pronouncing on the hypocrisies of society and religion, 'he is always lightly nervous about her' (K. Millett, 130). The novel appears to be centred around Jude, and Sue seems to be marginalized. A conventional view of Sue's relation to the narrator is that Hardy 'never commits himself to Sue as he did to Jude, and insists on seeing her obliquely or at a distance' (ib., 131).

For some (male) critics, Sue's apparent intellectual and emotional fluidity is womanly fickleness which 'teased us with obscure hints of an elusive meaningfulness'.[33] Is she pagan or Christian? Agnostic, atheist or believer? Sensual or chaste? Modernist or Hellenist? Sue's behaviour and views confuse the traditional critic, who would like to fix Sue in a particular socio-religious framework ('"[t]here's no order or regularity in your eccentricities, Sue"' complains Phillotson, IV. iii). Her intellectual fluidity seems to be as perplexing, to the old-fashioned critic, as the ambiguity and flow of postmodern texts. For example, as Robert Heilman points out, Sue buys the Classical statues, nearly repents of the act, then hides them and lies about them to her landlady (ib.). She enthusiastically and caustically criticizes the views of others but withers under criticism of her own views. 'She is cool about seeing Jude, then very eager, then offish' writes Heilman (ib., re. III, i).

Many Thomas Hardy critics have noted that Sue Bridehead is a talkative but elusive character. Indeed, the more she talks, the less the reader knows about her, the more absent she becomes. Like so many characters in fiction, Sue is seen largely through another character. For a long time the text only shows Sue through Jude's idealizing, desiring vision. As John Goode puts it, 'we never ask what is happening to Sue, it is Sue happening to Jude' (1979, 104). Sue is and is not like those characters that do not have a life outside of one character's views (E. Langland, 1980). When Jude is not thinking about or looking at her, Sue still 'exists'. However, Sue represents an ideological void in the text: the more she talks, the deeper the silence grows in the text.[34] Some of the time, Jude has no idea why Sue keeps leaving him, keeps retreating. For Jude, Sue is a riddle, a mass of contradictions, who resists critical analysis as well as Jude's questions. It is Sue who is 'obscure', not Jude (M. Jacobus, 1975).

Sue's destructivenes, D.H. Lawrence recognized, derives from her talkativeness, her insistence on 'subjecting… experience to the trials of language'; Sue 'utters herself – whereas in the ideology of sexism, the woman is an image to be uttered.'[35] Sue talks a lot (she is 'too articulate' [L. Williams, 1995, 191]), but utters a series of negatives which frustrates Jude, and other characters, endlessly.

Sue seems to be so articulate about every subject except herself. The one thing she will not submit to (psycho)analysis is herself. She is a compulsive analyzer of everything around her, but fails to find a social identity which will satisfy her many demands and requirements. Sue is clear about what or who she is not, but not about what/ who she is. Sue's social and ideological negativity relates directly to the notions of *différance* and alterity in French feminism, where, as Julia Kristeva said 'woman' is elsewhere, and Luce Irigaray wrote that 'woman' was 'other in herself': '[w]hen a girl begins to talk, she is already unable to speak of/to herself' (1991, 101).

For so long the reader views Sue through Jude's eyes: first as a long-lost cousin; then as a potential friend; then a lover; then a soul-mate; then a fickle, sometimes cold-blooded woman, and so on. And when Jude dies, Sue is not shown. It is a surprise, then to come across the times when Sue is seen alone, as when she buys the 'pagan' statues, or in chapter three of 'Part Four', 'At Shaston', where Sue is seen alone, unaccompanied by the usual mediation of Jude Fawley. Here we see Sue musing on the passionate kiss she has just enjoyed with Jude. However, Sue is still described in the sometimes harsh masculinist tones of the narrator, who calls her an 'ethereal, fine-nerved, sensitive girl' unable or unfitted to sleep with Phillotson or 'possibly with scarce any man' (IV. iii).

It's worth noting that when Sue Bridehead is first seen without Jude she comes across as not particularly ethereal or idealized. She simply goes on a walk out of Christminster and buys the statues from a gypsy (II. iii). Sue is not at all the nervy, repressed intellectual rebel that Jude sees.[36] Jude's sexism appears when, disappointed by women, he makes generalized statements about them, in an effort to distance himself from their grasp. When things become problematical between himself and Sue or Arabella, Jude resorts to being bemused and frustrated by 'woman'.

Even the narrator of *Jude the Obscure* seems confused by Sue's behaviour and personality. In the middle of the book the narrator describes Sue's thinking as 'extraordinarily compounded': what is OK in thought or theory becomes wrong in practice (IV. iii). The narrator implies that Sue might have interesting and liberal thoughts, but when the time comes to put them into practice, she balks. This occurs when she marries Phillotson: Jude reckons Sue hasn't thought it through, and 'rehearsing' it beforehand in the church is like a game to her. When Sue goes through the mock marriage with Jude before she marries Phillotson (ironically the only time she goes to the altar with Jude), he thinks she is being perverse, callous, unromantic, cruel. Are women 'more callous, and less romantic' than men, he wonders, 'or were they more heroic?' (III. vii). It is a question often asked by Hardy's male lovers.

In the short story *The Romantic Adventures of a Milkmaid* Margaret and Jim Hayward are married but not married. They are married, but they do not live together at first, echoing the themes of *Jude the Obscure*. '"We must suffer for our mistake"' says Margaret (SS, 1053). Margaret says what Sue Bridehead says, that marriage should be dissolvable if both parties are unhappy, something Hardy believed in deeply.

> "A thing can't be legal when it's against the wishes of the persons the laws are made to protect." (SS, 1049)

One of the most reactionary of Thomas Hardy's critics, Mrs Oliphant, who loathed *Jude the Obscure*, was right when she saw that Sue kept bringing sex into the foreground. Although Jude wants sex, it's Sue who keeps talking about it. Sue's actions, too, draw attention to her sexual identity and preoccupations (her sudden changes from 'acting' petulant and girl-like to being high-minded and moral, for example). Poor Jude, the masculinist Hardy critic thinks, being taken for a ride by such a flirt or teaser. Jude takes Sue so much at face value, and is consequently hurt by her shifts from intellectual rebel to tearful child. Arabella articulates this cynical view of Sue for the narrator. Jude contributes to the subjugation of Sue, too: he keeps calling her his 'dear little girl', for example, even though, at Aldbrickham, she is a pregnant woman in her late twenties. In exalting her, Jude also limits her, just as happened when figures such as the Virgin Mary were worshipped. Being put on a pedestal limits women, feminists have said.

In a way, Sue has to be so sexually repressed or 'fastidious' in order that Hardy's attack of Victorian morality and law could be as savage as he intended. If Sue had been sexually active in a more sensual (or 'acceptable') manner, the arguments may have been weakened (in the eyes of the Victorian moral establishment). Instead of presenting Sue as a sexually creative woman, Hardy's narrator etherealizes her through Jude's idealizing (yet lustful) gaze. The erotic look of the Hardy narrator in *Jude*, though, takes many opportunities to dwell on Arabella's sexuality, often drawing attention to her 'round and prominent bosom', just as the narrator of *Tess of the d'Urbervilles* continually eroticizes Tess's mouth.

Sue is in fact sexually active, though Thomas Hardy does not describe it directly, as he does with Arabella, but by metaphor and analogy. The Wessex Agricultural Show scene, although it is a public, daylit scene, where discussions of intimate matters like sex do not usually occur, offers the most vivid expression of Sue's sexual creativity. Arabella remarks to her companion Anny that Sue doesn't seem 'to know what love is – at last what I call love' (V. v). The reader assumes that Arabella is talking about sexual, orgasmic experience (R. Morgan, 1988, 149).

The text, though, offers a contrasting view here, for Sue is shown enjoying a multi-sensory experience. She is alive to the scents, sounds, sights and tastes of the Wessex Agricultural Show. Hardy's descriptions abounds with thinly veiled erotic allusions – 'the gay sights, the air, the music' which 'quickened her blood and made her eyes sparkle with vivacity' (V. v). And then there are the roses, not difficult to decipher symbolically (as with the roses that Alec d'Urberville presses upon Tess's breast). Sue is in an erotic bliss at the Agricultural Show. Sue's ecstasy – unexpected from Arabella's point of view – is partly what grates with Arabella, for she is saddled with a fat, alcoholic and violent bore for a husband.

Jude tells Sue that she is quite different from other women (what he means is, she won't sleep with him, or tell him she loves him). He calls her a '"phantasmal, bodiless creature"' who has '"so little animal passion"' in her (V. i). Later on, he tells Sue that he has '"danced attendance on [her] so long for such poor returns"' (V. ii).

Sue's views on sex continually perplex the male characters. For instance, Sue says she is called sexless or cold by some people, but asserts that '"[s]ome of the most passionately erotic poets have been the most self-contained in their daily lives"' (III. iv). This confuses the men in her life immensely: how, they wonder, can someone align themselves with the 'most passionately erotic poets' and yet not wish to put their erotic feelings into practice. To *say* one is erotic, and yet not to do anything with one's erotic feeling – it goes against Jude's – and Phillotson's – deepest instincts. Jude enjoys sex, and Sue tells him she is very sexual, yet she doesn't necessarily want to have sex. For Jude, Sue's sexuality is a mass of conflicting signals. For Sue, her sexuality doesn't need to be expressed, it is enough to be 'self-contained', chaste, pure within herself.

And when Sue does express her sexuality, it is still confusing to Jude. For example, he cannot understand her erotic intensity when Arabella returns, when Sue decides to sleep with him. For the reader, Jude is a substantial object, but Sue is more distanced, 'more removed into memory'; thus, '[a]s voyeurs, as pornographic readers of Sue, we maintain her hollowness and thus her desirability' (J. Kincaid, 139). At other times, Sue presents an ambiguous sexuality and gender – when she is dressed in his Melchester rooms in his clothes, and looks like his double. Sue eschews being fixed in any particular discourse or ideology. She will not be set down to one philosophy. 'She dodges brilliantly, and courageously creates for herself possibilities where we thought there were none' remarked James Kincaid (145). Sue, the intellectual and fastidious one, expresses an enjoyment in erotic poetry, which further confuses Jude. Sue says that the *Song of Songs* is a 'great and passionate song' of 'ecstatic, natural, human love' (III. iv). Sue despises the bishops or theologians who plastered over the *Song of Songs* with their 'ecclesiastical abstractions'. Christianity tried desperately to bring the *Song of Songs* into line with the rest of the *Bible*, and failed.

Sue is right, of course: the eroticism of the *Song of Songs* is intense, and superbly lyrical, and no amount of Pauline or Augustinian theological commentary can suppress its eroticism. The *Song of Songs* is, as Julia Kristeva says in her excellent analysis of it ("A Holy Madness: She and He", in *Tales of Love*), significant because it allows the female Shulamite lover as much expression as the male. 'The amorous dialogue is tension and *jouissance*, repetition and infinity; not as communication but as *incantation*. Song dialogue. *Invocation*' (1987, 93). Kristeva sees in the *Song of Songs* the deep-seated links between art and love, between love imagined and love 'real'. It's clear to Kristeva that the psychic or inner space of the *Song of Songs* is inseparable from the amorous space. Or vice versa, more accurately. What appears to be 'realistic' gestures and emotions are all manufactured and theatrical. Erotic desire energizes and drives the poem sequence, but it's art – that is, the imagination – that shapes and finishes the project.

> *As intersection of corporeal passion and idealization, love is undisputably the privileged experience for the blossoming of metaphor (abstract for concrete, concrete for abstract) as well as incarnation (the spirit becoming flesh, the word-flesh). Unless incarnation is a metaphor that has slipped into the real and has been taken for reality? A hallucination that is assumed to be real on account of the violence of amorous passion, which is in fact the ordinary manifestation of an alienation that confuses the fields of representation (real – imaginary – symbolic?).* ("A Holy Madness: She and He", 1987, 95)

Again, one thinks not only of the *Song of Songs*, to which Julia Kristeva is referring here, but also the history of love poetry from Ovid through Petrarch to Hardy and beyond. Kristeva rightly recognizes in the Shulamite of the *Song of Songs* one of the first appearances of a sovereign woman, someone who is the equal of her lover, who is 'limpid, intense, divided, quick, upright, suffering, hoping' (1987, 100). One thinks of Sue here. For Kristeva, the *Song of Songs* is fascinating because of 'its being a legitimation of the impossible, an impossibility set up as amatory law' (ib., 97). One can see how this would appeal to Hardy, for *Jude the Obscure*, in its evocation of a Platonic two-in-one love, is also about the 'impossibility' of love.

Of course, Hardy's use of the *Song of Songs* in a deeply ironic text like *Jude the Obscure* is full of irony. Sue's partial identification with the Shulamite in the *Song of Songs* inevitably reveals the shortcomings in real life. Love in real life can never be as ecstatic as in the *Song of Songs*; again, 'the letter killeth', because it sets up such waves of ecstasy that cannot be sustained or even found anywhere in 'real life'. Sue's striving towards the *Song of Songs* is seen as potentially damaging as Jude's enshrinement of philosophy and Christminster. Jude's retort to Sue's attack on the Church's censoring of the *Song of Songs* is that she is being 'Voltairean'. Jude uses the phrase again when Sue tells him that she doesn't '"regard marriage as a Sacrament"' (III. vi). This is deeply ironic, in view of what occurs later in the novel, and it also seems to contradict Sue's statements on the importance of 'ecstatic, natural, human love'.

"NOBODY IS EVER ON MY SIDE!": *JUDE THE OBSCURE* AND AFTER

In passages omitted from the *Life*, Thomas Hardy said that the criticisms of *Jude the Obscure* were 'outrageously personal, unfair and untrue'.[37] Some Hardy critics (Max Beerbohm, for example) have pointed out that such a powerful author as Hardy would not have been stopped from writing novels by a few reviews.[38] Other suggestions include the idea that Hardy would have made enough money from his fourteen novels to be able to devote himself to poetry (Michael Millgate, Charles Lock); further, Hardy knew that poetry and drama formed the core of 'great' literature – he did not have enough 'great' poetry by the mid-1890s, but his novels would do as far as literary merit went.

There are some tremendous lapses of style in *Jude the Obscure*, which perhaps helped the novel become, according to some critics, Thomas Hardy's worst (it has also been called his best too). For example, there is much weeping and fits of tears from Sue, and Jude. Describing Sue, Hardy writes: 'she blinked away an access of eye moisture', a typical illustration of Hardy's penchant for convoluted prose. The dialogue in *Jude the Obscure* is sometimes unbelievably trite, and banal. Sue's speech in particular is freighted with an amazing number of exclamation marks (in the 1912 Wessex edition), which makes her seem a breathless, excitable speaker. Sometimes the authorial voice cleverly manipulates the narrative. For example, after Sue has been 'rehearsing' getting married and is back with Phillotson she requests her 'lover' (referring to Jude) not to be a long time (III. vii). When Sue and Jude are falling in love, at Melchester, the dialogues are cut off, just when things are warming up. This is a classic technique of putting off fulfilment and thereby sustaining interest. But the lapses in prose style don't make any dint on the impact of *Jude the Obscure* as one of the most vehment and bitter attacks on contemporary society.

Jude the Obscure marks an astonishing finale to the series of novels that make Thomas Hardy one of the great fiction writers in the history of world literature.

NOTES

I   Introductory

1. J. Hillis Miller: "Steven's Rock and Criticism as Cure, II", *Georgia Review*, 30, 1976

2. Hélène Cixous: *Jours de l'an [First days of the year]*, 1990, in H. Cixous, 1994, 185

3. F.R. Leavis: "Hardy the Poet", *Southern Review*, 1940; *The Great Tradition*, London 1948

4. Patricia Stubbs, for example, writes that Hardy is 'almost unique in the English nineteenth-century novel, in that he creates women who are sexually exciting' (1979, 65).

II   Thomas Hardy and Feminism

1. Peter Widdowson writes:

Hardy, as we have him, is so inscribed with the processes of the consumption and reproduction of his work in history that it is now, as it were, a palimpsest of the perceptions, evaluations, readings, re-readings, and re-writings of a particular literary and æsthetic – not to say national – tradition. (1989, 57)

2. Sarah Kozloff: "Narrative Theory", in R. Allen: *Channels of Discourse*, Methuen, 1987, 55

3. Most Hardy criticism is distinctly patriarchal, it is 'based on a

reading determined by a dominant gender ideology', and there's no doubting that this bias is masculine (George Wotton, 183)

4. Donald Hall, "Afterword", *Tess of the d'Urbervilles*, Signet, New York 1964, 424

5. Judith Mitchell: "Hardy's Female Reader", in H, 178

6. Robert Kiely: "The Menace of Solitude: The Politics and Aesthetics of Exclusion in *The Woodlanders*", in H, 188

7. Luce Irigaray: "Sexual Difference", in T. Moi, 1987, 124

8. Judith Halberstam: "F2M: The Making of Female Masculinity", in L. Doan, 1994, 212

9. Sue Wilkinson & Celia Kitzinger; "Dire Straights?: Contemporary Rehabilitation of Heterosexuality", in G. Griffin, 1994, 84

10. Catherine MacKinnon: "Feminism, Marxism, Method, and the State: An Agenda for Theory", in N.O. Keohane, ed: *Feminist Theory: A Critique of Ideology*, Harvester, 1982

11. Critics such as A.O. Cockshut remain adamant: '[t]he attempt to turn Hardy into a feminist is altogether vain' (*Man and Woman: Love in the Novel 1740-1940*, Collins 1977, 129).

12. The sexual relations in Thomas Hardy's fiction, as in all fiction, occur within heteropatriarchal ideology. As Elizabeth Grosz writes, '[a]ll sexual practices...are made possible and function within the constraints of heterosexism and phallocentrism', but these are not perfect, immutable systems, Grosz asserts, 'they are contradictory systems, fraught with complexities, ambiguities, and vulnerabilities that can and should be used to strategically discern significant sites of contestation' ("Refiguring Lesbian Desire", in L. Doan, 1994, 69). Adrienne Rich, in "Compulsory Heterosexuality and Lesbian Existence", writes that 'gender inequality' also means 'the enforcement of heterosexuality for women as a means of assuring male right of physical, economical and emotional access' (1980).

13. Edwin Ardener: "Belief and the Problem of Women", in Shirley Ardener, ed: *Perceiving Women*, Halsted Press, New York 1978

14. H. Cixous, "The Laugh of the Medusa", in E. Marks, 254

15. Elaine Showalter writes:

We can think of the "wild zone" of women's culture spatially, experientially, or metaphysically. Spatially, it stands for an area which is literally no-man's land, a place forbidden to men... Experientially it stands for the aspects of the female life-style which are outside of and unlike those of men; again, there is a corresponding zone of male experience alien to women. But if we think of the wild zone metaphysically or in terms of consciousness, it has no corresponding male space since all of male consciousness is within the circle of the dominant structure and thus accessible to or structured by language.

Elaine Showalter: "Feminist Criticism in the Wilderness", in E. Showalter, 1986, 262-3; Jeanne Addison Roberts: *The Shakespearean Wild: Geography, Genus and Gender*, University of Nebraska Press, Lincoln, Nebraska 1991, 1-5

16. Sherry B. Ortner: "Is female to male as nature is to culture?", in M. Rosaldo & L. Lamphere, eds: *Woman, Culture and Society*, Stanford University Press 1974

17. Ann Rosalind Jones: "Writing the Body: L'Écriture féminine", in E. Showalter, 1986, 363

18. Victor Burgin: "Geometry and Abjection", in J. Fletcher, 1990, 115-6

19. L. Irigaray: *Ce sexe qui n'en est pas un*, Minuit, Paris 1977, 28-29

24. Luce Irigaray: "La différence sexuelle", *Ethiope de la différence sexuelle*, Minuit, Paris, 1984, and in Toril Moi, 1988, 128

21. Moira Gatens: "Power, Bodies and Difference", in T. Barrett, 1992, 134

22. J. Kristeva: "La femme, ce n'est jamais ça", *Tel Quel*, Autumn 1974, in E. Marks, 135

23. Hélène Cixous: "Sorties", in E. Marks, 95

24. J. Kristeva: *About Chinese Women*, 1977, 63

25. M. Duras, interview in *Signs*, Winter 1975, in E. Marks, 175

26. H. Cixous: "The Laugh of the Medusa", *Signs*, Summer 1976, in E. Marks, 249

27. Rachel DuPlessis: "For the Etruscans", in Showalter, 1986, 273

28. Mary Jacobus: "Is There a Woman in This Text?", in *New Literary Criticism*, Autumn, 1982, 14, 1

29. G. Spivak, 1990, 109. Emma Pérez: "Irigaray's Female Symbolic in the Making of Chicana Lesbian *Sitios y Lenguas (Sites and Discourses)*", in L. Doan, 108

30. T. Moi: *Sexual/ Textual Politics*, 139

31. See Susan Rubin Suleiman: "(Re)Writing the Body: The Politics of Female Eroticism", in *Risking Who One Is*, MIT Press 1995, 14f; Elizabeth Grosz: "Desire, the body and recent French feminism', *Intervention*, 21-2, 1988, 28-33; Alison M. Jagger & Susan R. Bordo, eds: *Gender/ Body/ Knowledge: feminist reconstructions of being and knowing*, Rutgers University Press, New Brunswick 1989; Naomi Schor, Naomi Schor: *Breaking the Chain: Women, Theory and French Realist Fiction*, New York 1985

32. Monique Witting: "One Is Not Born a Woman", speech at the Feminist as Scholar Conference, May 1979, Barnard College, New York

33. The phrases come from C. Schwichenberg: *The Madonna Connection: Representational Politics, Subcultural Identities and Cultural Theory*, Westview Press, Boulder, CO, 1993; R. Braidotti, *Patterns of Dissonance*, Polity, 1991; see L. Butler, 1990; S. Wilkinson in G. Griffin, 1994

34. Becky Rosa sees monogamy as an ideology which society encourages women to conform to by using 'cultural products (the media), economic restraints (tax incentives, the high cost of single living), social factors (the provision of support and companionship, or social status and privilege) and by the notion that this is 'how it is', 'this is natural' (B. Rosa, in G. Griffin, 1994, 107-8).

35. Christobel Mackenzie: "The Anti-Sexism Campaign Invites You to Fight Sexism, Not Sex", in A. Assiter, 1993, 144

36. John Kucich: "Moral Authority in the Late Novels: The Gendering of Art", in H, 234; P. Stubbs, 1981, 58f; P. Boumelha, 1982, 48

37. See Julia Kristeva: *Desire in Language*; *Révolution du language poétique*, Seuil, Paris 1974

38. Marxist-Feminist Literature Collective: "Women's Writing: *Jane Eyre, Shirley, Villette, Aurora Leigh*", in Francis Barker *et al*, eds: *1848: The Sociology of Literature*, in M. Eagleton, ed. *Feminist Literary Theory: A Reader*, 1979

39. J. Kristeva: *Women's Time*, in *The Kristeva Reader*, 208

40. J. Kristeva: *Histoires d'amour*, Denoël, Paris, 1983, and in *The Kristeva Reader*, 242

41. J. Kristeva: *Women's Time*, in *The Kristeva Reader*, 191

42. L. Irigaray: "The poverty of psychoanalysis", *The Irigaray Reader*, 101

43. Helena Michie makes this point in relation to Pierston in *The Well-Beloved*, in *The Flesh Made Word: Female Figures and Women's Bodies*, Oxford University Press 1987, 112

44. Luce Irigaray: *Speculum of the Other Woman*, tr. Gillian C. Gill, and *This Sex Which Is Not One*, tr. Catherine Porter, both Cornell University Press, New York 1985; see also: Dorothy Leland: "Lacanian psychoanalysis and French feminism: toward an adequate political psychology", *Hypatia*, 3 (3), Winter 1989, 81-103

45. Elizabeth Grosz: "Refiguring Lesbian Desire", in L. Doan, 75

46. R. Rilke, letter to Clara Rilke, 8 March 1907, in *Gesammalte Briefe 1892-1926*, Insel Verlag, Leipzig 1940, II, 279f

47. J. Lacan, "The meaning of the phallus", 1988; Bernard Baas: "Le désir pur", *Ornicar?*, 83, 1987.

48. C. Jung: *The Development of Personality*, vol. 17, Routledge, 1954, 198; Marie-Louise von Franz: *The Psychological Meaning of Redemption*

Motifs in Fairy Tales, Inner City Books, Toronto 1980, 39f

49. Emma Jung & Marie-Louise von Franz: *The Grail Legend, tr.* Andrea Dykes, Sigo Press, Boston, Mass., 1980, 64

50. Larysa Mykyta: "Lacan, Literature and the Look", *SubStance* (39), 1983, 54

51. Lady Jayne ad, *Clothes Show* magazine, December 1992

52. See Laura Mulvey: "Visual pleasure and narrative cinema", *Screen*, vol 16, no.3, 1975, 6-19

53. Kristin Brady: "Textual Hysteria: Hardy's Narrator on Women", in H, 1993, 89

54. Catherine King: "The Politics of Representation: A Democracy of the Gaze", in F. Bonner, 136

55. Luce Irigaray, "Women's Exile", in D. Cameron, 1990, 83; and Luce Irigaray: *Speculum.*

56. Dianne Fallon Sadoff: "Looking at Tess: The Female Figure in Two Narrative Media", in H, 151

57. Emma Pérez: "Irigaray's Female Symbolic in the Making of Chicana Lesbian *Sitios y Lenguas* (*Sites and Discourses*)", in L. Doan, 108

58. Hardy's letter to Alexander Macmillan, 25 July 1868, in M. M. Seymour-Smith, 1995, 85

59. Sappho, in *Greek Lyric Poetry*, ed. W. Barnstone, Schocken Books, New York 1977, 4

60. J. Keats, 'Ode to Melancholy', *Poems*, Oxford 1909, 141

61. P. Shelley, *Selected Poems*, Dent 1983, 163

62. Stendhal, *De l'Amour*, Penguin 1975

63. J. Kristeva: "In Praise of Love", in *Tales of Love*, 6

64. Paul Éluard wrote:

La vie sans cesse a recherche d'un novel amour, par effacer l'amour ancient, l'amour dangereux, la vie voulait changer d'amour. [Life unceasingly searching for a new love, to obliterate the old love, the dangerous love, life wanted to change love.] (From *Uninterrupted Poetry*, New Directions, New York 1975, 22-23)

65. Hélène Cixous: "Extreme Fidelity", in S. Sellers, 1988, and in H. Cixous, 1994, 132

66. H. Cixous, *(With) Ou l'art de l'innocence [(With) Or the art of innocence]*, 1981, in H. Cixous 1994, 95

67. Kristin Brady: "Textual Hysteria: Hardy's Narrator on Women", in H, 1993, 94

68. In her essay "Refiguring Lesbian Desire", Elizabeth Grosz describes

desire in post-Lacanian/ Hegelian terms which accords with desire in Hardy's fiction:

The only object desire can desire is an object that will not fill the lack or provide complete satisfaction. To provide desire with its object is to annihilate it. Desire desires to be desired. Thus, for Hegel, the only object that both satisfies desire yet perpetuates it is not an object but another desire... Desire is the movement of substitution that creates a series of equivalent objects to fill a primordial lack.

The mechanics of desire also have an economical dimension explored most fully in *Tess*. 'Now this notion of desire as an absence, lack, or hole, an abyss seeking to be engulfed, stuffed to satisfaction' continues Grosz,

is not only uniquely useful in capitalist models of acquisition, propriety, and ownership (seeing the object of desire on the model of the consumable commodity), but it also inherently sexualizes desire, coding it in terms of the prevailing characteristics attributed to the masculine/ feminine opposition, presence and absence. Desire, like female sexuality itself is insatiable, boundless, relentless, a gaping hole that cannot be filled or can only be temporarily filled; it suffers an inherent dependence on its object(s), a fundamental incompletion without them.' (E. Grosz, in L. Doan, 1994, 71)

69. Lawrence Durrell, *Sebastian*, 1983, 151

70. Bette Gordon & Karin Kay: "Look Back/ Talk Back", in P. Gibson, 1993, 91

71. John Kucich: "Moral Authority in the Late Novels: The Gendering of Art", in H, 224

72. B. Rich: "Compulsory Heterosexuality and Lesbian Existence", in B. Rich, 1980

73. Becky Rosa: "Anti-monogamy: A Radical Challenge to Compulsory Heterosexuality?", in G. Griffin, 1994, 110

74. Christobel Mackenzie: "The Anti-Sexism Campaign Invites You to Fight Sexism, Not Sex", in A. Assiter, 1993, 140

75. Claudia: "Fear of Pornography", in A. Assiter, 1993, 132

76. See Colleen Lamos: "The Postmodern Lesbian Position: *On Our Backs*", in L. Doan, 1994, 96; J. Butler, 1990; Case: "Toward a Butch-Femme Aesthetic", in Lynda Hart, ed: *Making a Spectacle: Feminist Essays on Contemporary Women's Theatre*, University of Michigan Press, Ann Arbor 1989

77. Becky Rosa: "Anti-monogamy: A Radical Challenge to Compulsory Heterosexuality?", in G. Griffin *et al*, 1993, 107

78. Bette Gordon & Karin Kay: "Look Back/ Talk Back", in P. Gibson, 1993, 95

79. Kristin Brady: "Textual Hysteria: Hardy's Narrator on Women", in H, 1993, 90

80. Janet Dixon: "Separatism", *Spare Rib*, 192, 1988, 6

81. See Alice, Gordon, Debbie and Mary: "Separatism", in S. Hoagland, 1988, 31-40; Ti-Grace Atkinson: *Amazon Odyssey*, Links Books, New York 1974; Sally Munt, 1992

82. M. Wittig: "One is not born a woman", in S. Hoagland, 446-7. Wittig's lesbian materialist analysis of heterosexuality (in *The Straight Mind*) ignores some of the ways in which 'compulsory heterosexuality' can be subverted in a postmodern era. (Cathy Griggers: "Lesbian Bodies in the Age of (Post)Mechanical Reproduction", in L. Doan, 1994, 124)

83. Daniel R. Schwarz: "Beginnings and Endings in Hardy's Major Fiction", in D. Kramer, 1979, 28

84. J. Kristeva: "Romeo and Juliet: Love-Hatred in the Couple", in *Tales of Love*, 225

85. S. Freud: "Drives and their vicissitudes", *Papers on Metapsychology*, 1915

86. J. Kristeva: "Narcissus: The New Insanity", in *Tales of Love*, 116

87. J. Kristeva: "Bataille and the Sun, or the Guilty Text", in *Tales of Love*, 368

88. Perry Meisel: "Interview with Julia Kristeva", tr. Margaret Waller, *Partisan Review*, no. 51, Winter 1984, 131-2

89. John Lechte: "Art, Love and Melancholy in the Work of Julia Kristeva", in J. Fletcher, 1990, 24

90. Camille Paglia, "Love Poetry", in A. Preminger & T. Bogan, eds: *The Princeton Encyclopedia of Poetry and Poetics*, Princeton University Press 1993

III   *Jude the Obscure*

1. In "Pornography and Male Supremacy", Andrea Dworkin writes that '[k]idnapping, or rape, is also the first known form of marriage – called "marriage by capture"' (1988, 229).

2. See Daniel Schwarz: "Beginnings and Endings in Hardy's Major Fiction", in D. Kramer, 1979, 33f; P. Casagrande, 1982, 203; D. Sonstroem, 1981, 9; A. Friedman, 1966, 71f

3. Terry Eagleton sees *Jude the Obscure* as a 'calculated assault' on the reader, a deliberate flouting of the laws of realism. (T. Eagleton:

"Introduction", *Jude the Obscure*, Macmillan, 1974)

4. 'It is true to say of him that, at his greatest, he gives us impressions; at his weakest, arguments... In *Jude the Obscure* argument is allowed to dominate impression, with the result that though the misery of the book is overwhelming, it is not tragic.' (V. Woolf, *the Common Reader*, in R. Draper, 1975, 76-77)

5. At the same time, although *Jude* is a novel of psycho-social displacement, it is curiously static, and much of it is a series of essentially dialogue scenes concerning marriage, taking place in one room (or on one stage set).

6. For example, Susan Brownmiller: *Against Our Will: Men, Women and Rape*, Bantam, New York, 1976; Barbara Toner: *The Facts of Rape*, Arrow 1977; K. Millett, 1970; Christine Delphy: *The Main Enemy: A Materialist Analysis of Women's Oppression*, Women's Research and Resources Centre, 1977; E. Wilson: *Women and the Welfare State*, Tavistock 1977; Susan Griffin: *Pornography and Silence: Culture's Revenge Against Nature*, Women's Press 1981; Shulamith Firestone: *The Dialectic of Sex*, Women's Press, 1979

7. Elizabeth Langland: "Becoming a Man: *Jude the Obscure*", in H, 1993, 35

8. Robert Schweik: "The 'Modernity' of Hardy's *Jude the Obscure*", in P. Mallett, 53

9. Robert Rehder writes that the 'tragedy in Hardy's novels is often the end of a dream. The awakening is a prelude to destruction' (in L. Butler, 1977, 24).

10. How harsh Hardy is in *Jude the Obscure*, describing Jude's nighttime entry into his long-beloved Christminster, listening to the ghosts of the intellectual city, and brushing his work-hardened hands over the walls and carvings of the colleges. (It is interesting to compare the young Jude's entry into his New Jerusalem with that of the seventeen-year-old J.M.W. Turner's: 'Sunday July 22.92. Left London in Evening reached Oxford at 3 in the morning – which was delightfully clear and the stillness of the scene gave additional solemnity to the venerable assemblage of Gothic buildings in this City.' (J.M.W. Turner: *Collected Correspondence of J.M.W. Turner*, ed. John Gage, Clarendon Press 1980, 11) Both young men fell in love with the city – Turner, typically, languishing in the visual atmosphere, while the Hardyan anti-hero feels the philosophical ghosts of the Past blowing coldly through him.

11. T. Hardy, letter to Edmund Gosse, 20 November 1895, in R. Draper, 1975, 34

12. H. Cixous, "Sorties", in E. Marks, 1981, 90f

13. See Robert Hollander: *Boccaccio's Two Venuses*, Columbia University Press 1977, 4

14. The physical side of love is crucial, however, for when a kiss does occur, as when Sue is leaving Shaston, it is 'a turning-point in Jude's career' (IV. iii).

15. 'There has never been a more intense communication of desire' (Warner, 1985, 126)

16. Patricia Ingham: "Provisional Narratives: Hardy's Final Trilogy", in L. Butler 1989, 56

17. T. Hardy, quoted in F. Pinion, 1992, 245

18. Edmund Gosse, review in *St James's Gazette*, November 1895

19. T. Hardy, 20 November 1895, in the Norton *Jude*, 349-350

20. Avedon Carol & Nettie Pollard: "Changing Perception in the Feminist Debate", in A. Assiter, 1993, 52

21. Rosemary Sumner suggests that Hardy was not quite ready to depict strugggles of sexuality as well as spirit or psychology. 'This, perhaps, is the novel which would have followed *Jude* if he had written another; this, perhaps, is why it was never written.' (1981, 165) But Hardy had been depicting sexual torment from his first outings into fiction, and, by *The Woodlanders*, could state, in the preface, that his intention was to explore sexual relations between men and women (39).

22. H. Cixous, "The Laugh of the Medusa", in E. Marks, 256; Irigaray, *Speculum*, in Irigaray, 1991, 59; Gauthier, "Pourquoi Sorcières", in E. Marks, 201

23. Phillotson comes round to Sue's grim way of thinking, which is close to that of Hardy's narrators, throughout his fiction. Regaled by Arabella's blunt polemic on being rough to flighty women, Phillotson says: '"[c]ruelty is the law pervading all nature and society; and we can't get out of it if we would!"' (V. viii)

24. D.H. Lawrence wrote:

> *It is the same cry all through Hardy, this curse upon the birth in the flesh, and this unconscious adherence to the flesh. The instincts, the bodily passions are strong and sudden in all Hardy's men. They are too strong and sudden. They fling Jude into the arms of Arabella, years after he has known Sue, and against his own will. (Study of Thomas Hardy, in 1971, 219)*

Jude's sleeping with Arabella, though, may be simply instinctual lust, but Jude knows how he is failing himself, as well as Sue. As Sue says of Jude, rightly: '"[y]our theories are not as advanced as your practice."' (173)

25. James Kincaid: "Hardy's Absences", in D. Kramer, 1979, 205

26. David Lodge is typical among masculinist critics in his assessment of Arabella: '[t]hat there is something coarse, degrading and, to a fastidious sensibility, disgusting about Arabella's sexuality, is suggested by her close association with, of all animals, pigs.' "*Jude the Obscure*: Pessimism and Fictional Form", in D. Kramer, 1979, 198

27. In the *Harper's* serial, this speech was extended: '"I don't see why society shouldn't be reorganized on a basis of Matriarchy – the woman and the children being the unit without the man, and the men to support the women and children collectively – not individually, as we do now."' (*Harper's*, European edition, 30, 125)

Hardy was sympathetic to the suffragette movement. 'I have for a long time been in favour of women-suffrage' he wrote in an unpublished letter to the Fawcett Society, written in 1906. He went on to discus his women-centred notions, which Phillotson proposed in *Jude the Obscure*:

> *I am in favour of it because I think the tendency of the women's vote will be to break up the present pernicious conventions in respect of women, customs, religion, illegitimacy, the stereotyped household (that it must be the unit of society), the father of a woman's child (that it is anybody's business but the woman's own)...* (in R. Sumner, 1981, 190)

28. Janet Dixon: "Separatism", *Spare Rib*, 192, 1988, 6

29. See Alice, Gordon, Debbie and Mary: "Separatism", in S. Hoagland, 1988, 31-40; Ti-Grace Atkinson: *Amazon Odyssey*, Links Books, New York 1974; Sally Munt, 1992

30. M. Wittig: "One is not born a woman", in S. Hoagland, 1988, 446-7

31. For example, here's one from a mid-1990s newspaper:

> *A six-year-old boy found hanged in his bedroom was the victim of a tragic accident while playing on his own, police said. His mother found him entangled in a dressing gown cord and tried to revive him at their home in Chelmsford, Essex.*

("Boy, 6, dies in hanging tragedy", *The Independent*, 22 October 1995)

32. Elizabeth Langland: "Becoming a Man: *Jude the Obscure*", in H, 1993, 46

33. Robert Heilman: "*Jude the Obscure*", *Nineteenth-Century Fiction*, 20, 1966

34. H.C. Duffin, in his 1916 book on Hardy, said that there was something unsolvable in *Jude the Obscure*, some enigma that eludes the reader (*Thomas Hardy*, Manchester 1964, 77).

35. John Goode, 1979, 101; L. Williams, 1995, 191

36. Grace Melbury is seen as full of 'modern nerves' and Sue is seen as 'fine-nerved'; in Victorian times bourgeois women were viewed by the medical profession as suffering from primarily three diseases: neurasthenia, chlorosis and hysteria. These diseases were seen as being nearly always related to sexual reproduction. (P. Boumelha, 1982, 37)

37. T. Hardy, in November 1895, in Per, 242

38. M. Beerbohm, in E.J. Brenneke: *The Life of Thomas Hardy*, New York 1925, 191

BIBLIOGRAPHY

All books are published in London, England, unless otherwise stated.

Thomas Hardy

Jude the Obscure, ed. Patricia Ingham, Oxford University Press 1985
Jude the Obscure: An Authoritative Text, Backgrounds and Sources, Criticism, ed. Norman Page, W.W. Norton & Co, New York 1978
Tess of the D'Urbervilles, ed. David Skilton, Penguin 1978/85
Tess of the D'Urbervilles: An Authoritative Text, Hardy and the Novel, ed. Scott Elledge, W.W. Norton & Co, New York 1965/79
Tess of the d'Urbervilles, eds. Juliet Grindle & Simon Gatrell, Oxford University Press 1983
Tess of the d'Urbervilles, World Classics, eds. Juliet Grindle & Simon Gatrell, Oxford University Press 1988
"Tess of the d'Urbervilles", Graphic, XLIV, July-December 1891
The Return of the Native, ed. George Woodcock, Penguin 1978
The Woodlanders, ed. James Gibson, Penguin 1981
The Mayor of Casterbridge, ed. Martin Seymour-Smith, Penguin 1985
Under the Greenwood Tree, ed. Simon Gatrell, Oxford University Press 1985
A Pair of Blue Eyes, ed. Alan Manford, Oxford University Press 1985
The Well-Beloved, ed. Tom Hetherington, Oxford University Press 1986
Two on a Tower, ed. F.B. Pinion, Macmillan 1975
A Laocidean, Heron/Macmillan 1987
The Hand of Ethelberta, ed. Robert Gittings, Macmillan 1975

The Trumpet-Major, St Martins Library, Macmillan 1962
Complete Poems, ed. James Gibson, Macmillan 1981
Selected Poems, ed. Walford Davies, Dent 1982
Selected Short Poems, ed. John Wain, Macmillan 1966/75
The Gates Along the Path: Poems, Terra Nova Editions 1979
Hardy's Love Poems, ed. Carl J. Weber, Macmillan 1983
The Short Stories of Thomas Hardy, Macmillan 1928
The Literary Notebooks of Thomas Hardy, ed. Lennart A. Björk, 2 vols, Macmillan 1985
The Collected Letters of Thomas Hardy, eds. Richard Little Purdy & Michael Millgate, 7 vols, Clarendon Press 1978-88
Thomas Hardy's Notebooks, ed. Evelyn Hardy, Hogarth Press 1955
The Personal Notebooks of Thomas Hardy, ed. Richard H. Taylor, Macmillan 1978
The Life of Thomas Hardy, Macmillan 1962
The Life and Work of Thomas Hardy, ed. Michael Millgate, Macmillan 1984
Personal Writings, ed. Harold Orel, Macmillan 1967

Others

Gary Adelman: *Jude the Obscure: A Paradise of Despair*, Twayne, New York 1992
John Alcorn: *The Nature Novel from Hardy to Lawrence*, Macmillan 1973
Patricia Alden: *Social Mobility in the English Bildungsroman*, UMI Research Press, Ann Arbor 1986
B.J. Alexander: "Anti-Christian Elements in Thomas Hardy's Novels", *DAI*, 36, 1975
Wayne Anderson: "The Rhetoric of Silence in Hardy's Fiction", *Studies in the Novel*, 17, 1985
Alison Assister & Avedon Carol, eds: *Bad Girls and Dirty Pictures: The Challenge to Reclaim Feminism*, Pluto Press 1993
D.F. Barber, ed. *Concerning Thomas Hardy*, Charles Skilton 1968
J.O. Bailey: *The Poetry of Thomas Hardy*, University of North Carolina Press, Chapel Hill 1970
Regina Barreca, ed: *Sex and Death in Victorian Literature*, Indiana University of California Press, Bloomington 1990

John Barrell: "Geographies of Hardy's Wessex", *Journal of Historical Geography*, 8, 1982

John Bayley: *An Essay on Hardy*, Cambridge University Press 1978

Philippa Berry & Andrew Wernick, eds: *Shadow of Spirit: Postmodernism and Religion*, Routledge 1992

Kathleen Blake: "Pure Tess: Thomas Hardy on Knowing a Woman", *Studies in English Literature*, 22, 1982

Paula Blank: "*Tess of the d'Urbervilles*": The English Novel and the Foreign Plot", *Mid-Hudson Language Studies*, 12, 1989

Harold Bloom, ed: *Thomas Hardy: Modern Critical Views*, Chelsea House, New York 1987

E. Blunden. *Thomas Hardy*, London, 1942

Charlotte Bonica: "Nature and Paganism in Hardy's *Tess*", *Journal of English Literary History*, 49, 4 1982

F. Bonner *et al*, eds. *Imagining Women Cultural Representations and Gender*, Polity Press, Cambridge, 1992

Penny Boumelha: *Thomas Hardy and Women: Sexual Ideology and Narrative*, Harvest 1982

A. Brick. "Paradise and Consciousness in Hardy's *Tess*", *19th Century Fiction*, 17, 1962

Jean Brooks: *Thomas Hardy: The Poetic Structure*, Elek 1971

B. Brown & P. Adams: "The feminine body and feminist politics", *M/F*, 3, 1979

Douglas Brown: *Thomas Hardy*, Longmans, Green & Co. 1954

S.H. Brown: ""Tess" and Tess: An Experiment in Genre", *Modern Fiction Studies*, 28, 1, 1982

J.H. Buckley: "Tess and the d'Urbervilles", *Victorian Institute Journal*, 20, 1992

J.B. Bullen: *The Expressive Eye: Fiction of Perception in the Work of Thomas Hardy*, Clarendon Press 1986

Peter J. Burgard, ed: *Nietzsche and the Feminine*, University Press of Virginia, Charlottesville, 1994

Judith Butler: *Gender Trouble: Feminism and the Subversion of Identity*, Routledge 1990

Lance St. John Butler, ed. *Thomas Hardy, After Fifty Years*, Macmillan 1977

— *Thomas Hardy*, Cambridge University Press 1978

— ed. *Alternative Hardy*, Macmillan 1989

Elizabeth Campbell: "*Tess of the d'Urbervilles*: Misfortune Is a Woman", *Victorian Newsletter*, 70, 1989

Glen Cavaliero: *The Rural Tradition in the English Novel 1900-1939*,

Macmillan 1977

Joseph Campbell: *The Power of Myth,* with Bill Moyers, ed. Betty Sue Flowers, Doubleday, New York 1988

Richard Carpenter: *Thomas Hardy,* Macmillan 1978

Peter J. Casagrande: *Unity in Thomas Hardy's Novels,* Regents, Lawrence, 1982

— *Tess of the d'Urbervilles: Unorthodox Beauty,* Twayne, New York 1992

David Cecil: *Hardy the Novelist,* Constable 1943

R. Chapman: *The Language of Thomas Hardy,* Macmillan 1990

Gail Chester & Julienne Dickey, ed: *Feminism and Censorship: The Current Debate,* Prism Press, Bridport, Dorset 1988

Mary Childers: "Thomas Hardy, the Man Who 'Liked' Women", *Criticism,* 23, 1981

Hélène Cixous: *The Hélène Cixous Reader,* ed. Susan Sellers, Blackwell 1994

— *The Newly Born Woman,* tr. Betsy Wing, Minnesota University Press, Minneapolis 1986

Laura Claridge: "Tess: A Less Than Pure Woman Ambivalently Presented", *Texas Studies in Literature and Language,* 28, 3, 1986

— & Elizabeth Langland, eds: *Out of Bounds: Male Writers and Gender(ed) Criticism,* University Massachusetts Press, Amherst 1990

Vere H. Collins: *Talks With Thomas Hardy at Max Gate,* Duckworth 1972

W.V. Costanzo: "Polanski in Wessex: Filming *Tess of the d'Urbervilles",* *Literature/ Film Quarterly,* 9, 2, 1981

J. Stevens Cox, ed: *Thomas Hardy Yearbook,* Toucan Press, various dates

R.G. Cox, ed. *Thomas Hardy: The Critical Heritage,* Barnes & Noble 1970

Gail Cunningham: *The New Woman and the Victorian Novel,* Macmillan 1978

H.M. Daleski: "*Tess*: Mastery and Abandon", *Essays in Criticism,* 30, 1980

Jagdish Chandra Dave: *The Human Predicament in Hardy's Novels,* Macmillan 1985

Mary E. Chase: *Thomas Hardy From Serial to Novel,* University of Minnesota Press

Donald Davie: *Thomas Hardy and British Poetry,* Routledge & Kegan Paul 1979

Lois Deacon & Terry Coleman: *Providence and Mr. Hardy,* Hutchinson 1966

D. De Laura. "The Ache of Modernism in Hardy's Later Novels", Sept, 1967

Laura Doan, ed: *The Lesbian Postmodern,* Columbia University Press, New

York 1994

Mary Ann Doane: *The Desire to Desire: The Woman's Film of the 1940's*, Macmillan 1987

Margaret Drabble, ed. *The Genius of Thomas Hardy*, Weidenfeld & Nicolson, 1976

—ed. *A Writer's Britain*, Thames & Hudson 1979

R.P. Draper, ed. *Thomas Hardy: Three Pastoral Novels*, Macmillan 1987

—ed. *Hardy: The Tragic Novels*, Macmillan 1975

H.C. Duffin: *Thomas Hardy*, Greenwood Press, Conn., 1978

Andrea Dworkin: *Intercourse*, Arrow 1988

—*Pornography: Men Possessing Women*, Women's Press 1984

Mary Eagleton, ed: *Feminist Literary Criticism*, Longman 1991

Terry Eagleton: "Thomas Hardy: Nature as Language", *Critical Quarterly*, Summer 1971

Roger Ebbatson: *Lawrence and the Nature Tradition*, Harvester Press, Brighton 1980

—"The Plutonic Master: Hardy and the Steam Threshing Machine", *Critical Survey*, 2, 1990

—*Hardy: The Margin of the Unexpressed*, Sheffield Academic Press 1994

Ralph W.V. Elliott: *Thomas Hardy's English*, Basil Blackwell 1984

A. Enstice: *Thomas Hardy*, London 1979

R. Evans: "The Other Eustacia", *Novel*, 1, 1968

Joe Fisher: *The Hidden Hardy*, Macmillan 1992

Alexander Fischler: "Gins and Spirits: The Letter's Edge in Hardy's *Jude the Obscure*", *SNNTS*, 16, 1984

John Fletcher & Andrew Benjamin, ed: *Abjection, Melancholia and Love: the Work of Julia Kristeva*, Routledge 1990

John Fowles & Jo Draper: *Thomas Hardy's England*, Cape 1984

Janet Freeman: "Ways of Looking at Tess", *Studies in Philology*, 79, 3, 1982

Alan Friedman: *The Turn of the Novel*, Oxford University Press 1966

—ed: *Forms of Modern Fiction*, Austin 1975

Lorraine Gamman & Margaret Marshment, eds. *The Female Gaze: Women as Viewers of Popular Culture*, Women's Press 1988

Marjorie Garson: *Hardy's Fables of Integrity: Woman, Body, Text*, Oxford University Press 1991

Simon Gatrell: *Hardy the Creator: A Textual Biography*, Clarendon Press 1988

—*Thomas Hardy and the Proper Study of Mankind*, Macmillan 1993

—ed: *The Thomas Hardy Archive 1: Tess of the d'Urbervilles*, Garland, New York 1986

Helmut E. Gerber: & W. Eugene Davis, eds: *Thomas Hardy: An Annotated Bibliography of Writings About Him*, Northern Illinois University Press 1973

James Gibson & Trevor Johnson, eds. *Thomas Hardy: Poems: A Casebook*, Macmillan 1979

Pamela Church Gibson & Roma Gibson, eds: *Dirty Looks: Women, Pornography, Power*, British Film Institute 1993

Robert Gittings: *The Older Hardy*, Heinemann 1978

John Goode: "Sue Bridehead and the New Woman", in M. Jacobus, 1979

— *Thomas Hardy: The Offensive Truth*, Basil Blackwell 1988

W. Goetz: "Felicity and Infelicity of Marriage in *Tess of the d'Urbervilles*", *Nineteenth Century Fiction*, 38, 1983

William Greenslade: *Degeneration, Culture and the Novel 1880-1940*, Cambridge 1994

Ian Gregor: *The Great Web*, Faber 1974

J. Gribble. "The Quiet Women of Egdon Heath", *Essays In Criticism*, 46, 1996

Gabriele Griffin *et al*, eds: *Stirring It: Challenges For Feminism*, Taylor & Francis 1994

Elizabeth Grosz: *Sexual Subversions*, Allen & Unwin 1989

— *Volatile Bodies*, Indiana University Press, Bloomington 1994

Peter Grundy: "Linguistics and Literary Criticism: A Marriage of Convenience", *English*, 30, 137, 1981

Albert J. Guerard: *Thomas Hardy*, Oxford University Press 1949

— ed. *Hardy: A Collection of Critical Essays*, Prentice-Hall International, New York 1963/86

F.E. Halliday: *Thomas Hardy,* Adams & Dart, Bath 1972

G. Handley: *Thomas Hardy: Tess of the d'Urbervilles*, Penguin Critical Studies, Penguin 1991

T. Hands, T. *Thomas Hardy: Distracted Preacher?*, London, 1989

— . *A Hardy Chronology* London, 1992

— . *Thomas Hardy*, Macmillan, London, 1995

Margaret Harris: "Thomas Hardy's *Tess of the d'Urbervilles*: Faithfully presented by Roman Polanski", *Sydney Studies in English*, 7, 1982

G. Harvey. *The Complete Critical Guide To Thomas Hardy*, Routledge, London, 2003

M.E. Hassett: "Compromised Romanticism in *Jude the Obscure*", *Nineteenth Century Fiction*, 25, 1971

Desmond Hawkins: *Hardy's Wessex*, Macmillan 1983

— *Hardy: Novelist and Poet*, David & Charles, Devon 1976

Jeremy Hawthorn, ed: *The Nineteenth-Century British Novel*, Arnold 1986

Stephen Hazell, ed. *The English Novel,* Macmillan 1978

J. Hazen: "The Tragedy of Tess Durbeyfield", *Texas Studies in Literature and Language,* 11, 1969

R. Heilman: "Hardy's Sue Bridehead", *Nineteenth Century Fiction,* 20, 1966

Susan J. Hekman: *Gender and Knowledge: Elements of a Postmodern Feminism,* Polity Press 1990

Lucille Herbert: "Hardy's Views on Tess of the d'Urbervilles", *English Literary History,* 37, 1970

Margaret R. Higonnet, ed: *The Sense of Sex: Feminist Perspectives on Hardy,* University of Illinois Press, Urbana 1993

—"Fictions of Feminine Voice: Antiphony and Silence in Hardy's *Tess of the d'Urbervilles*", in L. Claridge 1990

G.G. Hiller, ed: *Poems of the Elizabethan Age,* Methuen 1977

Sarah Lucia Hoagland & Julia Penelope, eds: *For Lesbians Only: A separatist anthology,* Onlywomen Press 1988

Bert G. Hornback: *The Metaphor of Chance: Vision and Technique in the Works of Thomas Hardy,* Ohio University Press, Athens 1971

Irving Howe: *Thomas Hardy,* Macmillan 1985

Maggie Humm: *Feminisms: A Reader,* Harvester Wheatsheaf, 1992

—ed: *The Dictionary of Feminist Theory,* Harvester Wheatsheaf 1995

Virginia R. Hyman: *Ethical Perspectives in the Novels of Thomas Hardy,* Kenniket Press, New York 1975

Patricia Ingham: *Thomas Hardy,* Harvester Wheatsheaf, Hemel Hempstead 1989

Luce Irigaray: *The Irigaray Reader,* ed. Margaret Whitford, Blackwell, Oxford 1991

—*Je, tu, nous: Toward a Culture of Difference,* tr. Alison Martin, Routledge 1993

—*Thinking the Difference: For a Peaceful Revolution,* Athlone Press, 1994

—*Speculum of the Other Woman,* tr. G.C. Gill, Cornell University Press, New York 1985

—*This Sex Which Is Not One,* tr. C. Porter & C. Burke, Cornell University Press, New York, 1977

Arlene M. Jackson: *Illustration and the Novels of Thomas Hardy,* Macmillan 1981

Mary Jacobus: "Sue the Obscure", *Essays in Criticism,* 25, 1975

—"Tess's Purity", *Essays in Criticism,* 26, 1976

—ed: *Women Writing and Writing About Women,* Croom Helm 1979

—"Tess: The Making of a Pure Woman", in Bloom 1987

—"Hardy's Magian Retrospective", *Essays in Criticism,* 32, 1982

– *Reading Woman: essays in feminist criticism*, Methuen 1986

Trevor Johnson: *Thomas Hardy*, Evans Brothers, 1968

Ann Rosalind Jones: "Writing the Body: Toward an Understanding of L'Écriture féminine", in E. Showalter,1986

Denis Kay-Robinson: *The Landscape of Thomas Hardy*, Webb & Bower 1987

– *Hardy's Wessex Reappraised*, David & Charles, Newton Abbot, Devon 1972

W.J. Keith: *Regions of the Imagination: The Development of the British Rural Tradition*, University of Toronto Press, Toronto 1988

– *The Poetry of Nature: Rural Perspectives in Poetry From Wordsworth to the Present*, University of Toronto Press, Toronto 1980

A. Kettle. *Hardy the Novelist*, University of Wales Press, Swansea, 1967

James Kincaid: "Hardy's Absences", in D. Kramer, 1979

Dale Kramer: *Thomas Hardy: The Forms of Tragedy*, Macmillan 1975

– ed: *Critical Approaches to the Fiction of Thomas Hardy*, Barnes, Totowa, 1979

– ed: *Critical Essays on Thomas Hardy: The Novels*, G.K Hall 1990

– *Tess of the d'Urbervilles*, Cambridge University Press 1991

–. ed. *The Cambridge Companion to Thomas Hardy*, Cambridge University Press, Cambridge, 1999

Julia Kristeva: *Desire in Language: A Semiotic Approach to Literature and Art*, ed. Leon Roudiez, tr. Thomas Gora, Alice Jardine & Leon Roudiez, Blackwell 1982

– *The Kristeva Reader*, ed. Toril Moi, Blackwell 1986

– *Tales of Love*, tr. Leon S. Roudiez, Columbia University Press, New York 1987

– *About Chinese Women*, tr. A. Barrows, Boyars 1977

– *Powers of Horror: An Essay on Abjection*, tr. Leon S. Roudiez, Columbia University Press, New York 1982

– *Revolution in Poetic Language*, tr. Margaret Walker, Columbia University Press, New York 1984

– "A Question of Subjectivity: an interview" [with Susan Sellers], *Women's Review*, 12, 1986, in P. Rice, 1992

Weston La Barre: *The Ghost Dance*, Allen & Unwin 1972

– *Muelos*, Columbia University Press, New York 1985

Jacques Lacan and the *Ecole Freudienne: Feminine Sexuality*, ed. Juliet Mitchell and Jacqueline Rose, Macmillan 1982

J.T. Laird: *The Shaping of "Tess of the d'Urbervilles"*, Oxford University Press 1975

– "New Light on the Evolution of *Tess of the d'Urbervilles*", *Review of*

English Studies, 31, 124, 1980

Elizabeth Langland: "A Perspective of One's Own: Thomas Hardy and the Elusive Sue Bridehead", *Studies in the Novel*, 12, 1980

—*Gothic Manners and the Classic English Novel*, University of Wisconsin Press, Madison 1988

—"Masculinity in *Jude the Obscure*", in M. Higonnet 1993

Albert J. LaValley, ed. *Tess of the D'Urbervilles: A Collection of Critical Essays*, Prentice-Hall, New Jersey 1969

D.H. Lawrence: *Study of Thomas Hardy and Other Essays*, ed. Bruce Steele, Cambridge University Press 1985

—*A Selection from Phoenix*, ed. A.A.H. Inglis, Penguin 1971

— *Selected Essays*, Penguin 1950

— *The Rainbow*, ed. John Worthen, Penguin 1981/6

—*The Complete Short Novels*, ed. Keith Sagar & Melissa Partridge, Penguin 1982/7

—*Aaron's Rod*, Penguin 1950

— *Sons and Lovers*, ed. Keith Sagar, Penguin 1981/6

—*Kangaroo*, Penguin 1950

Herman Lea: *Thomas Hardy's Wessex*, Macmillan 1977

Glenda Leeming: *Who's Who in Thomas Hardy*, Elm Tree 1975

Lawrence Lerner & John Holmstrom: *Thomas Hardy and His Readers*, Bodley Head 1968

Charles Lock: *Thomas Hardy: Criticism in Focus*, Bristol Classic Press 1992

David Lodge: *Language of Fiction*, Routledge & Kegan Paul 1966

Bryan Longhrey, ed: *Critical Survey*, Thomas Hardy number, 5, 2, 1983

Jakob Lothe: "Hardy's Authorial Narrative Methods in *Tess of the d'Urbervilles*", in J. Hawthorn 1986

John Lucas: *The Literature of Change*, Harvester 1977

Phillip V. Mallett & Ronald P. Draper, eds: *A Spacious Vision: Essays on Hardy*, Patten Press, Penzance 1994

Jane Marcus: "A Tess For Child Molesters", *Jump Cut*, 3, 1981

S. Marcus. *The Other Victorians*

Elaine Marks & Isabelle de Courtivron, eds: *New French Feminisms: an anthology*, Harvester Wheatsheaf 1981

Karl Marx, *Selected Works*, I, Lawrence & Wishart 1942

Helena Michie: *The Flesh Made Word: Female Figures and Women's Bodies*, Oxford University Press 1987

Ruth Milberg-Kaye: *Thomas Hardy: Myths of Sexuality*, John Jay Press, New York 1983

R. Miles. "The Women of Wessex", in A. Smith, 1979

J. Hillis Miller: *Thomas Hardy: Distance and Desire*, Oxford University

Press 1970

—*Fiction and Repetition: Seven English Novels*, Harvard University Press 1982

Kate Millett: *Sexual Politics*, Doubleday, Garden City 1970

Michael Millgate: *Thomas Hardy: His Career as a Novelist*, Bodley Head 1971

—*Thomas Hardy: A Biography*, Oxford University Press 1982

Sara Mills *et al*, eds. *Feminist Readings/ Feminists Reading*, University Press of Virginia, Charlottesville 1989

—. ed. *Gendering the Reader*, Harvester Wheatsheaf 1993

W. Mitsichelli: "Androgyny, Survival, and Fulfilment in Thomas Hardy's *Far From the Madding Crowd*", *Modern Language Studies*, 18, 3, 1988

Toril Moi: *Sexual/Textual Politics: Feminist Literary Theory*, Routledge 1988

—ed: *French Feminist Thought*, Blackwell 1988

Rosemarie Morgan: *Women and Sexuality in the Novels of Thomas Hardy*, Routledge 1988

Roy Morrell: *Thomas Hardy: The Will and the Way*, University of Malaysia Press, 1965

R.D. Morrison: "Reading and Restoration in *Tess of the d'Urbervilles*", *Victorian Newsletter*, 82, 1992

Sally Munt, ed: *New Lesbian Criticism: Literary and Cultural Readings*, Harvester Wheatsheaf 1992

Timothy O'Sullivan: *Thomas Hardy: An Illustrated Biography*, Macmillan 1981

Norman Page, ed: *Thomas Hardy: The Writer and His Background*, Bell & Hyman 1980

—ed: *Thomas Hardy Annual*, Macmillan, 1983-

—& Peter Preston, eds: *The Literature of Place*, Macmillan 1993

B. Paris: ""A Confusion of Many Standards": Conflicting Value Systems in *Tess of the d'Urbervilles*", *Nineteenth Century Fiction*, 24, 1970

Lynn Parker: ""Pure Woman" and Tragic Heroine? Conflicting Myths in Hardy's *Tess of the d'Urbervilles*", *Studies in the Novel*, 24, 1992

J. Paterson: *The Making of 'The Return of the Native'*, University of California Press 1960

Michael Payne: *Reading Theory: An Introduction to Lacan, Derrida, and Kristeva*, Blackwell 1993

John Peck: *How to Study a Thomas Hardy Novel*, Macmillan 1983

Charles P.C. Petit, ed: *New Perspectives on Thomas Hardy*, Macmillan 1994

F.B. Pinion: *A Hardy Companion*, Macmillan 1968

—ed: *Thomas Hardy and the Modern World*, Thomas Hardy Society,

Dorchester 1974

— *Thomas Hardy: Art and Thought*, Macmillan 1977

Monique Plaza: ""Phallomorphic power" and the psychology of "woman"", *Ideology and Consciousness*, 4, 1978

M. Ponsford: "Thomas Hardy's Control of Sympathy in *Tess of the d'Urbervilles*", *Midwest Quarterly*, 27, 1986

Adrian Poole: "Men's Words and Hardy's Women", *Essays in Criticism*, 31, 1981

C.L. Preston: *A KWIC Concordance to Thomas Hardy's Tess of the d'Urbervilles*, Garland, New York 1989

R.L. Purdy: *Thomas Hardy: A Bibliography Study*, Oxford University Press 1954

Lyn Pykett: "Ruinous bodies: women and sexuality in Hardy's late fiction", in B. Longhrey 1983

John Rabbets: *From Hardy to Faulkner: Wessex to Yoknapatawpha*, Macmillan 1989

M. Ray. *Thomas Hardy*, Ashgate, Aldershot, 1997

Philip Rice & Patricia Waugh, eds: *Modern Literary Theory: A Reader*, Arnold 1992

Adrienne Rich: *Blood, Bread and Poetry*, Virago 1980

— *Of Woman Born: Motherhood as Experience and Institution*, Virago 1977

Jeanne Addison Roberts: *The Shakespearean Wild: Geography, Genus and Gender*, University of Nebraska Press, Lincoln, Nebraska 1991

Katharine Rogers: "Women in Thomas Hardy", *Centennial Review*, 19, 1975

C.H. Salter: *Good Little Thomas Hardy*, Macmillan 1981

Nadine Schoenburg: "The Supernatural in *Tess*", *Thomas Hardy Yearbook*, 19, 1989

Arthur Schopenhauer: *Essays and Aphorisms*, Penguin 1970

Martin Seymour-Smith: *Hardy*, Bloomsbury 1994

Charles Shapiro, ed: *Twelve Original Essays on Great English Novels*, Detroit 1960

G.W. Sherman: *The Pessimism of Thomas Hardy*, Associated University Press, New Jersey 1976

Elaine Showalter, ed: *The New Feminist Criticism*, Virago 1986

Kaja Silverman: "History, Figuration and Female Subjectivity in *Tess of the d'Urbervilles*", *Novel*, 18, 1984

— *The Acoustic Mirror: The Female Voice in Psychoanalysis and Cinema*, Indiana University Press, Bloomington 1988

Anne Smith, ed. *The Novels of Thomas Hardy*, Vision Press 1979

J. Sommers: "Hardy's other *Bildungsroman: Tess*", *English Literature in*

Transition, 25, 1982

David Sonstroem: "Order and Disorder in *Jude the Obscure*", *English Literature in Transition*, 24, 1981

F.R. Southerington: *Hardy's Vision of Man*, Chatto & Windus 1971

Dale Spender: *The Writing or the Sex? why you don't have to read women's writing to know it's no good*, Pergamon Press, New York 1989

Marlene Springer: *Hardy's Use of Allusion*, Macmillan 1983

R.W. Stallamn: "Hardy's Hour-Glass Novel", *Sewanee Review*, 55, 1947

Patricia Stubbs: *Women and Fiction: Feminism and the Novel, 1880-1920*, Harvester, 1979

Rosemary Sumner: *Thomas Hardy: Psychological Novelist*, Macmillan 1981

T. Tanner. "Colour and Movement in Hardy's *Tess of the d'Urbervilles*", *Critical Quarterly*, 10, 1968

Dennis Taylor: *Hardy's Poetry, 1860-1928*, Macmillan 1981

— "The Second Hardy", *Sewanee Review*, 96, 1988

Richard H. Taylor: *The Neglected Hardy*, Macmillan 1982

Charlotte Thompson: "Language and the Shape of Reality in *Tess of the d'Urbervilles*", *English Literary History*, 50, 4, 1983

Eric Tridgill: *Madonnas and Magdalens: The Origins and Development of Victorian Sexual Attitudes*, Heinemann 1976

Christopher Walbank: *Thomas Hardy*, Blackie, Glasgow 1979

Nell K. Waldman: ""All that she is": Hardy's Tess and Polanski's", *Queen's Quarterly*, 88, 3, 1981

Marina Warner: *Alone Of All Her Sex: The Myth and Cult of the Virgin Mary*, Picador 1985

Valerie Wayne, ed: *The Matter of Difference: Materialist Feminist Criticism of Shakespeare*, Harvester Wheatsheaf 1991

Harvey Webster: *On a Darkling Plain*, University of California Press 1947

Judith Weissman: "The Deceased Wife's Sister Marriage Act and the Ending of *Tess of the d'Urbervilles*", *American Notes and Queries*, 14, 1976

Ottis Wheeler: "Four Versions of *The Return of the Native*", *Nineteenth Century Fiction*, 14, 1959

R.J. White: *Thomas Hardy and History*, Macmillan 1974

Margaret Whitford: *Luce Irigaray: Philosophy in the Feminine*, Routledge 1991

G. Glen Wickens: "Victorian Theories of Language and *Tess of the d'Urbervilles*", *Mosaic*, 19, 1986

Peter Widdowson: *Hardy in History: A study in literary sociology*, Routledge 1989

— *D.H. Lawrence*, Longman 1992

—ed: *Thomas Hardy: Tess of the d'Urbervilles: New Casebooks*, Macmillan 1993

—. ed. *Thomas Hardy*, Palgrave Macmillan, London, 1996

Jonathan Wike: "The World as Text in Hardy's Fiction", *Nineteenth Century Literature*, 47, 1993

Linda Ruth Williams: *Critical Desire: Psychoanalysis and the Literary Subject*, Arnold 1995

—*Sex in the Head*, Harvester Wheatsheaf, 1995

Merryn Williams: *Thomas Hardy and Rural England*, Macmillan 1972

—*A Preface to Hardy*, Longman 1976

Judith Wittenberg: "Angels of Vision and Questions of Gender in *Far From the Madding Crowd*", *The Centennial Review*, 31, 1, 1968

—"Thomas Hardy's First Novel: Women and the Quest for Autonomy", *Colby Library Quarterly*, 18, 1982

—"Early Hardy Novels and the Fictional Eye", *Novel*, 16, 1983

Monique Wittig: *The Lesbian Body*, tr. David Le Vay, Beacon Press, Boston 1986

—*The Straight Mind*, Beacon Press, Boston 1992

George Wootton: *Thomas Hardy: Towards a Materialist Criticism*, Barnes & Noble, Goldenbridge 1985

Terence Wright: *Tess of the d'Urbervilles*, Macmillan 1987

—*Hardy and the Erotic*, Macmillan 1989

Jack Zipes: *Don't Bet on the Prince: Contemporary Feminist Fairy Tales in North America and England*, Methuen, New York 1986

J.R.R. Tolkien
The Books, The Films, The Whole Cultural Phenomenon

by Jeremy Mark Robinson

A new critical study of J.R.R. Tolkien, creator of Middle-earth and author of *The Lord of the Rings, The Hobbit* and *The Silmarillion,* among other books.

This new critical study explores Tolkien's major writings (*The Lord of the Rings, The Hobbit, Beowulf: The Monster and the Critics, The Letters, The Silmarillion* and *The History of Middle-earth* volumes); Tolkien and fairy tales; the mythological, political and religious aspects of Tolkien's Middle-earth; the critics' response to Tolkien's fiction over the decades; the Tolkien industry (merchandizing, toys, role-playing games, posters, Tolkien societies, conferences and the like); Tolkien in visual and fantasy art; the cultural aspects of The Lord of the Rings (from the 1950s to the present); Tolkien's fiction's relationship with other fantasy fiction, such as C.S. Lewis and *Harry Potter;* and the TV, radio and film versions of Tolkien's books, including the 2001-03 Hollywood interpretations of *The Lord of the Rings.*

This new book draws on contemporary cultural theory and analysis and offers a sympathetic and illuminating (and sceptical) account of the Tolkien phenomenon. This book is designed to appeal to the general reader (and viewer) of Tolkien: it is written in a clear, jargon-free and easily-accessible style.

754pp   ISBN 1-86171-057-7   £25.00 / $37.50

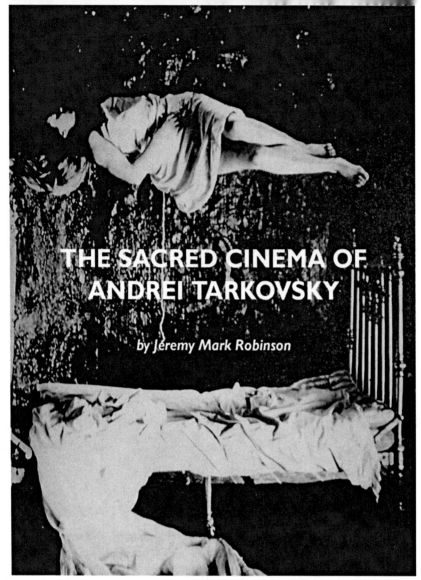

THE SACRED CINEMA OF ANDREI TARKOVSKY

by Jeremy Mark Robinson

A new study of the Russian filmmaker Andrei Tarkovsky (1932-1986), director of seven feature films, including *Andrei Roublyov, Mirror, Solaris, Stalker* and *The Sacrifice*.

This is one of the most comprehensive and detailed studies of Tarkovsky's cinema available. Every film is explored in depth, with scene-by-scene analyses. All aspects of Tarkovsky's output are critiqued, including editing, camera, staging, script, budget, collaborations, production, sound, music, performance and spirituality. Tarkovsky is placed with a European New Wave tradition of filmmaking, alongside directors like Ingmar Bergman, Carl Theodor Dreyer, Pier Paolo Pasolini and Robert Bresson.

An essential addition to film studies.

Illustrations: 150 b/w, 4 colour. 682 pages. First edition. Hardback.

Publisher: Crescent Moon Publishing. Distributor: Gardners Books.

ISBN 1-86171-096-8 (9781861710963) £60.00 / $105.00

The Best of Peter Redgrove's Poetry
The Book of Wonders

by Peter Redgrove, edited and introduced by Jeremy Robinson

Poems of wet shirts and 'wonder-awakening dresses'; honey, wasps and bees; orchards and apples; rivers, seas and tides; storms, rain, weather and clouds; waterworks; labyrinths; amazing perfumes; the Cornish landscape (Penzance, Perranporth, Falmouth, Boscastle, the Lizard and Scilly Isles); the sixth sense and 'extra-sensuous perception'; witchcraft; alchemical vessels and laboratories; yoga; menstruation; mines, minerals and stones; sand dunes; mud-baths; mythology; dreaming; vulvas; and lots of sex magic. This book gathers together poetry (and prose) from every stage of Redgrove's career, and every book. It includes pieces that have only appeared in small presses and magazines, and in uncollected form.

'Peter Redgrove is really an extraordinary poet' (George Szirtes, *Quarto* magazine) 'Peter Redgrove is one of the few significant poets now writing... His 'means' are indeed brilliant and delightful. Technically he is a poet essentially of brilliant and unexpected images...he never disappoints' (Kathleen Raine, *Temenos* magazine).

240pp   ISBN 1-86171-063-1   2nd edition   £19.99 / $29.50

Sex–Magic–Poetry–Cornwall
A Flood of Poems

by Peter Redgrove. Edited with an essay by Jeremy Robinson

A marvellous collection of poems by one of Britain's best but underrated poets, Peter Redgrove. This book brings together some of Redgrove's wildest and most passionate works, creating a 'flood' of poetry. Philip Hobsbaum called Redgrove 'the great poet of our time', while Angela Carter said: 'Redgrove's language can light up a page.' Redgrove ranks alongside Ted Hughes and Sylvia Plath. He is in every way a 'major poet'. Robinson's essay analyzes all of Redgrove's poetic work, including his use of sex magic, natural science, menstruation, psychology, myth, alchemy and feminism.
A new edition, including a new introduction, new preface and new bibliography.

'Robinson's enthusiasm is winning, and his perceptive readings are supported by a very useful bibliography' (*Acumen* magazine)
'*Sex-Magic-Poetry-Cornwall* is a very rich essay... It is like a brightly-lighted box. (Peter Redgrove)
'This is an excellent selection of poetry and an extensive essay on the themes and theories of this unusual poet by Jeremy Robinson' (*Chapman* magazine)

220pp   New, 3rd edition   ISBN 1-86171-070-4   £14.99 / $23.50

THE ART OF ANDY GOLDSWORTHY

COMPLETE WORKS: SPECIAL EDITION
(PAPERBACK and HARDBACK)

by William Malpas

A new, special edition of the study of the contemporary British sculptor, Andy Goldsworthy, including a new introduction, new bibliography and many new illustrations.

This is the most comprehensive, up-to-date, well-researched and in-depth account of Goldsworthy's art available anywhere.

Andy Goldsworthy makes land art. His sculpture is a sensitive, intuitive response to nature, light, time, growth, the seasons and the earth. Goldsworthy's environmental art is becoming ever more popular: 1993's art book *Stone* was a bestseller; the press raved about Goldsworthy taking over a number of London West End art galleries in 1994; during 1995 Goldsworthy designed a set of Royal Mail stamps and had a show at the British Museum. Malpas surveys all of Goldsworthy's art, and analyzes his relation with other land artists such as Robert Smithson, Walter de Maria, Richard Long and David Nash, and his place in the contemporary British art scene.

The Art of Andy Goldsworthy discusses all of Goldsworthy's important and recent exhibitions and books, including the *Sheepfolds* project; the TV documentaries; *Wood* (1996); the New York Holocaust memorial (2003); and Goldsworthy's collaboration on a dance performance.

Illustrations: 70 b/w, 1 colour. 330 pages. New, special, 2nd edition.
Publisher: Crescent Moon Publishing. Distributor: Gardners Books.

ISBN 1-86171-059-3 (9781861710598) (Paperback) £25.00 / $44.00

ISBN 1-86171-080-1 (9781861710802) (Hardback) £60.00 / $105.00

ARTS, PAINTING, SCULPTURE

The Art of Andy Goldsworthy: Complete Works(Pbk)
The Art of Andy Goldsworthy: Complete Works (Hbk)
Andy Goldsworthy in Close-Up (Pbk)
Andy Goldsworthy in Close-Up (Hbk)
Land Art: A Complete Guide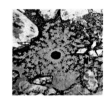
Richard Long: The Art of Walking
The Art of Richard Long: Complete Works (Pbk)
The Art of Richard Long: Complete Works (Hbk)
Richard Long in Close-Up
Land Art In the UK
Land Art in Close-Up
Installation Art in Close-Up
Minimal Art and Artists In the 1960s and After
Colourfield Painting
Land Art DVD, TV documentary
Andy Goldsworthy DVD, TV documentary
The Erotic Object: Sexuality in Sculpture From Prehistory to the Present Day
Sex in Art: Pornography and Pleasure in Painting and Sculpture
Postwar Art
Sacred Gardens: The Garden in Myth, Religion and Art
Glorification: Religious Abstraction in Renaissance and 20th Century Art
Early Netherlandish Painting
Leonardo da Vinci
Piero della Francesca
Giovanni Bellini
Fra Angelico: Art and Religion in the Renaissance
Mark Rothko: The Art of Transcendence
Frank Stella: American Abstract Artist
Jasper Johns: Painting By Numbers
Brice Marden
Alison Wilding: The Embrace of Sculpture
Vincent van Gogh: Visionary Landscapes
Eric Gill: Nuptials of God
Constantin Brancusi: Sculpting the Essence of Things
Max Beckmann
Egon Schiele: Sex and Death In Purple Stockings
Delizioso Fotografico Fervore: Works In Process 1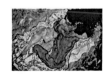
Sacro Cuore: Works In Process 2
The Light Eternal: J.M.W. Turner
The Madonna Glorified: Karen Arthurs

LITERATURE

J.R.R. Tolkien: The Books, The Films, The Whole Cultural Phenomenon
Harry Potter
Sexing Hardy: Thomas Hardy and Feminism
Thomas Hardy's *Tess of the d'Urbervilles*
Thomas Hardy's *Jude the Obscure*
Thomas Hardy: The Tragic Novels
Love and Tragedy: Thomas Hardy
The Poetry of Landscape in Hardy
Wessex Revisited: Thomas Hardy and John Cowper Powys
Wolfgang Iser: Essays
Petrarch, Dante and the Troubadours
Maurice Sendak and the Art of Children's Book Illustration
Andrea Dworkin
Cixous, Irigaray, Kristeva: The *Jouissance* of French Feminism
Julia Kristeva: Art, Love, Melancholy, Philosophy, Semiotics and Psychoanalysis
Hélene Cixous I Love You: The *Jouissance* of Writing
Luce Irigaray: Lips, Kissing, and the Politics of Sexual Difference
Peter Redgrove: Here Comes the Flood
Peter Redgrove: Sex-Magic-Poetry-Cornwall
Lawrence Durrell: Between Love and Death, East and West
Love, Culture & Poetry: Lawrence Durrell
Cavafy: Anatomy of a Soul
German Romantic Poetry: Goethe, Novalis, Heine, Hölderlin, Schlegel, Schiller
Feminism and Shakespeare
Shakespeare: Selected Sonnets
Shakespeare: Love, Poetry & Magic
The Passion of D.H. Lawrence
D.H. Lawrence: Symbolic Landscapes
D.H. Lawrence: Infinite Sensual Violence
Rimbaud: Arthur Rimbaud and the Magic of Poetry
The Ecstasies of John Cowper Powys
Sensualism and Mythology: The Wessex Novels of John Cowper Powys
Amorous Life: John Cowper Powys and the Manifestation of Affectivity (H.W. Fawkner)
Postmodern Powys: New Essays on John Cowper Powys (Joe Boulter)
Rethinking Powys: Critical Essays on John Cowper Powys
Paul Bowles & Bernardo Bertolucci
Rainer Maria Rilke
In the Dim Void: Samuel Beckett
Samuel Beckett Goes into the Silence
André Gide: Fiction and Fervour
Jackie Collins and the Blockbuster Novel
Blinded By Her Light: The Love-Poetry of Robert Graves
The Passion of Colours: Travels In Mediterranean Lands
Poetic Forms
The Dolphin-Boy

POETRY

The Best of Peter Redgrove's Poetry
Peter Redgrove: Here Comes The Flood
Peter Redgrove: Sex-Magic-Poetry-Cornwall
Ursula Le Guin: Walking In Cornwall
Dante: Selections From the Vita Nuova
Petrarch, Dante and the Troubadours
William Shakespeare: Selected Sonnets
Blinded By Her Light: The Love-Poetry of Robert Graves
Emily Dickinson: Selected Poems
Emily Brontë: Poems
Thomas Hardy: Selected Poems
Percy Bysshe Shelley: Poems
John Keats: Selected Poems
D.H. Lawrence: Selected Poems
Edmund Spenser: Poems
John Donne: Poems
Henry Vaughan: Poems
Sir Thomas Wyatt: Poems
Robert Herrick: Selected Poems
Rilke: Space, Essence and Angels in the Poetry of Rainer Maria Rilke
Rainer Maria Rilke: Selected Poems
Friedrich Hölderlin: Selected Poems
Arseny Tarkovsky: Selected Poems
Arthur Rimbaud: Selected Poems
Arthur Rimbaud: A Season in Hell
Arthur Rimbaud and the Magic of Poetry
D.J. Enright: By-Blows
Jeremy Reed: Brigitte's Blue Heart
Jeremy Reed: Claudia Schiffer's Red Shoes
Gorgeous Little Orpheus
Radiance: New Poems
Crescent Moon Book of Nature Poetry
Crescent Moon Book of Love Poetry
Crescent Moon Book of Mystical Poetry
Crescent Moon Book of Elizabethan Love Poetry
Crescent Moon Book of Metaphysical Poetry
Crescent Moon Book of Romantic Poetry
Pagan America: New American Poetry

MEDIA, CINEMA, FEMINISM and CULTURAL STUDIES

J.R.R. Tolkien: The Books, The Films, The Whole Cultural Phenomenon
Harry Potter
Cixous, Irigaray, Kristeva: The *Jouissance* of French Feminism
Julia Kristeva: Art, Love, Melancholy, Philosophy, Semiotics and   Psychoanalysis
Luce Irigaray: Lips, Kissing, and the Politics of Sexual Difference
Hélene Cixous I Love You: The *Jouissance* of Writing
Andrea Dworkin
'Cosmo Woman': The World of Women's Magazines
Women in Pop Music
Discovering the Goddess (Geoffrey Ashe)
The Poetry of Cinema
The Sacred Cinema of Andrei Tarkovsky (Pbk and Hbk)
Paul Bowles & Bernardo Bertolucci
Media Hell: Radio, TV and the Press
An Open Letter to the BBC
Detonation Britain: Nuclear War in the UK
Feminism and Shakespeare
Wild Zones: Pornography, Art and Feminism
Sex in Art: Pornography and Pleasure in Painting and Sculpture
Sexing Hardy: Thomas Hardy and Feminism

In my view *The Light Eternal* is among the very best of all the material I read on Turner. (Douglas Graham, director of the Turner Museum, Denver, Colorado)

The Light Eternal is a model monograph, an exemplary job. The subject matter of the book is beautifully organised and dead on beam. (Lawrence Durrell)

It is amazing for me to see my work treated with such passion and respect. (Andrea Dworkin)

Sex-Magic-Poetry-Cornwall is a very rich essay... It is like a brightly-lighted box. (Peter Redgrove)

CRESCENT MOON PUBLISHING
P.O. Box 393, Maidstone, Kent, ME14 5XU, United Kingdom.
01622-729593 (UK) 01144-1622-729593 (US) 0044-1622-729593 (other territories)
cresmopub@yahoo.co.uk   www.crescentmoon.org.uk

Printed in the United Kingdom
by Lightning Source UK Ltd.
132820UK00001B/271/P